OCCY

a Surfer's Year

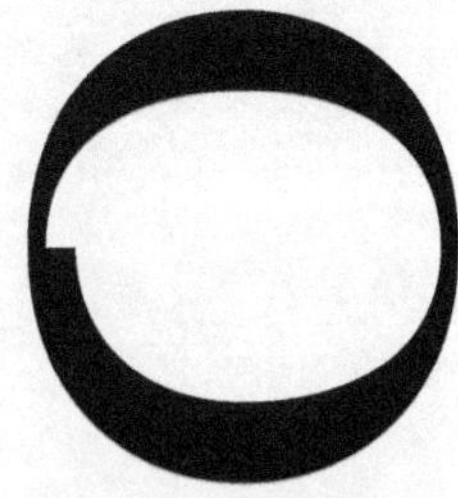

Mark Occhilupo with Sarge

a Surfer's Year

HarperSports
An imprint of HarperCollinsPublishers

Harper*Sports*
An imprint of HarperCollins*Publishers*, Australia

First published in Australia in 2000
by HarperCollins*Publishers* Pty Limited
ABN 36 009 913 517
A member of the HarperCollins*Publishers* (Australia) Pty Limited Group
www.harpercollins.com.au

HarperCollins*Publishers*
25 Ryde Road, Pymble, Sydney NSW 2073, Australia
31 View Road, Glenfield, Auckland 10, New Zealand
77–85 Fulham Palace Road, London W6 8JB, United Kingdom
2 Bloor Street East, 20th Floor, Toronto, Ontario M4W 1A8, Canada
10 East 53rd Street, New York NY 10022, USA

National Library of Australia Cataloguing-in-Publication data:

Occhilupo, Mark, 1966- .
A surfer's year.
ISBN 978-0-7322-6855-8
1. Occhilupo, Mark, 1966- . 2. Surfers - Australia - Biography.
I. Sargeant, Paul, 1955- . II. Title.
797.32092

Cover photographs: Sarge
Internal stock photographs: Sarge

Cover and internal design by Melanie Calabretta, HarperCollins Design Studio

dedication

I'D LIKE TO DEDICATE THIS BOOK
to my parents and sisters. I wouldn't have achieved what I have without their love and support. My father, Luciano, passed away ten years ago. I hope he's proud of me. My mother, Pam, drove me to every contest I ever wanted to go to, and just gave me total love and encouragement. Thanks Mum, and thanks also to my big sisters Alex, Fleur and Shanla.
Go the Occhilupos!

acknowledgments

ACKNOWLEDGMENTS? This whole project acknowledges the magic, brilliance, humour and utter honesty of one of Australia's greatest sporting heroes, Marco Luciano Occhilupo. Certainly I have never known anyone like him. It is thoroughly unlikely that there will ever be a more flamboyant and charismatic character in the history of pro surfing. He is an enchanted spirit, a pure soul, a national treasure. From redefining the limits and pure essence of surfing as a teenager in the 1980s, and then struggling through a cauldron of emotional unrest and personal issues to reemerge almost ten years later, still on the cutting edge, and claim a world title, he has proven that there is no such word as 'can't'. He has dragged so many of us along in his incredible wake, continually stunning and delighting us all with everything from his determination to his wit to his whimsical mastery of the world's waves. He made my career, he made companies, he made the last 20 years of professional surfing unforgettable. I salute him.

I first met Mark Occhilupo back in 1979, when he was 14. I don't know why, but somehow, God threw his life and mine into the same melting pot. My life was never the same again, inevitably drawn into the whirlpool of adventure and spirit that is professional surfing. I have been blessed to be there with him, to share, to watch, and to grow alongside two-plus generations of surfing athletes. What an amazing mission, but oh, what a joy it has been!

After 21 years of willing on my young friend Occy, I was devastated not to be in Rio last year to share that incredible moment when he clinched the crown he always so richly deserved. I never doubted his gift, his mission or his destiny. In a way, I'm glad I wasn't in Brazil. I honestly don't think I would have survived the utter stoke of it. I swear I would have had a heart attack. Though most will think me unstable at best, I honestly don't feel that the 1999 crown will be Occy's last world surfing triumph. He is the freak of freaks and, in my heart, I feel he's not done yet.

While history was being made in Brazil last October, I was stranded in London, unable to get a flight. Two hours before learning of Occy's unexpected conquest — well, at least at that time or place — I learnt that our mutual Cronulla friend Andrew Murphy had died back in Sydney. So when I heard the news of Occy's win, I was unable to react. I was distraught, angry and happy all at the same time. Two days later I finally got on a plane to Sydney, landing just in time to go to Murph's massive funeral service, before jumping on another plane to Coolangatta to celebrate Occy's world title win with him. It was the biggest emotional rollercoaster of my life.

As Occ and I sat in a bar in Figueira da Foz, Portugal, in mid September this year, recording his recollection of that crowning day in Rio, I cried tears of proud joy. Before then I had never really shared the moment with him. Even now, a few days later in the same place, as I sit at my computer typing these acknowledgments to put this monster to bed, tears run down my cheeks again. Yes, they are happy tears celebrating my friend's conquest and ongoing campaign, but they are also tears of sorrow for Murph and our other fallen friends from this crazy mixed-up life that we pursue. How they would have loved to see Occy finish the job. Though it is Occy's privilege to dedicate this book, I personally dedicate my contribution to it to those friends and pro surfing brothers that are no longer out there in the waves. May Andrew Murphy, Matt Smith, Peter Crawford, Sean Fanning, Joel Green, Ronnie Burns, Todd Chesser, Donnie Solomon and Mark Sainsbury all rest easy in the eternal barrel.

Never before have I put a book together but, as massive a task as it has been, it has proven an absolute pleasure and privilege, and I thank Occy for his time and sharing, as well as for the opportunity and honour of shepherding his words into print. Personally, I'd also like to thank those people who have supported me for so long, through so much, including my mum and my three younger brothers, and their families, my treasured friends and 'adopted family' the Mitchells, my Christian brother and counsel Craig Cleaver, my Cronulla mates (the 'Nulla is still the centre of my universe), as well as my travelling brothers and family on the ASP Tour. I also thank and honour the thousands of surfers who have treated me so well although I have never deserved to be part of their anointed world. I have been blessed.

In completing this project I would also like to thank the project coordinator Richard Yonge, Lahela Hatchett and Lucy Palmer for their help with transcribing the hours and hours of interview tape, my mate Aaron Blakey for getting the photos together,

Al Hunt for filling in our statistical memory gaps, as well as the crew at HarperCollins. Thanks also to the staff at *Tracks* and *Waves* for briefly allowing me to place their deadlines on the sideboard in order to complete this book, and to my young friend and apprentice Johan de Niet, who travelled and worked with me through the European 2000 leg and tolerated my being totally engrossed and consumed by this mission.

Most of all I would like to praise and thank my Lord and Saviour Jesus Christ for blessing me with this task in the first place, as well as providing me with the energy and spirit to complete the mission. All glory to Him! Finally, through this book, I trust you enjoy sharing the highs and lows of our times and trials on the international pro surfing road. Attempting to describe both our lifestyle and my friend The Ockster, I have to use that old phrase, 'It doesn't get any better!'

GODblessya (… even more), Sarge

contents

introduction

THE BEST YEAR EVER — SO FAR

1999! THE YEAR OF THE BULL! I was really psyched as soon as 1999 turned the corner. I remember thinking to myself on New Year's Eve how big and all-consuming the goal was that I'd set myself. The mission would start the following morning. I wanted to be the last world surfing champion of the millennium, and I *knew* I could do it.

I spent New Year's Eve '99 at home. We had a great party, and that was about the last of the partying for me, because I was really psyched. I woke up on 1 January and straight away I was ready to go. It was my first conscious thought of the year. I was *so* psyched! I went into some heavy training down at the back beach at Fingal, just *pounding* the beach. I'd thrust a stick in the sand where I turned around and every subsequent day I'd run a bit further down the beach. By the end of my two-month program I was running almost all the way from Fingal down to Kingscliff and back, which is over four kilometres each way. I was averaging at least five kilometres, in soft sand under a hot summer sun, which meant about 90 minutes of hard sweat and slog every day.

When the time came for the opening Billabong Pro WCT event on the Gold Coast, the swell was disappointingly small, and we

found ourselves at Cabarita down on the Tweed. Cabarita is a beautiful place, but it's not Burleigh or Kirra. I was still really amped though, and we had quite good waves considering the conditions. I had a really good board that I was happy with, and so I was halfway there. When I got my singlet for my first heat, I was just so ready to surf. I almost always wear wetsuits rather than shorts, but on this occasion I put on some really nice shorts. I was running down to the judges' tower to check-in and I remember seeing Bruce Lee, the Billabong team manager, watching me run down. Maybe it was just my imagination, but I'm sure he did a double take as he saw how fit and trimmed down I was. I wanted to show everyone how fit and psyched I was, as well as how good I was surfing. I had a good heat and won my first round convincingly in front of a good weekend crowd down there at Caba', thereby skipping the second round and advancing straight into the third.

In the third round I had Brazilian rookie Cristiano Spirro in a late afternoon heat, but somehow I seemed to be going the wrong way and pushing against the grain. Spirro is a pretty good surfer, and grovelled his way through before punching through the lip something like ten times on this one wave. Straightaway I had a good wave, and got an 8.5. I didn't need much thereafter. As fit as I was, I steamed back out, trying to force myself through the low tide's waves thumping on the bank, but I didn't get out there. It was only 4–5', but it was hard to get back out the back. I was bummed.

I walked away from that first contest with just a 17th placing, which obviously wasn't up to my expectations. Even though it was the first event of the season, I was spewing and it was way too early to be thinking like that. It wasn't just to do with my aspirations for the year, either. I've always wanted to do well in the Billabong Pro at home on the Goldy, but I never have. I had a few drinks that night but I was high on being fit, so I was up early and on with the training again the next morning.

I then went over to West Oz for the Margaret River WQS. I had the contest on a string, right through the whole event, and was stoked with how many people were coming up to me and telling me how good I was surfing. I was psyching for a win, and I made the final, but my travelling partner Luke Egan won.

At Bells the following week, I had a really good campaign and made it to the semi-finals, where I was eventually defeated by Sunny Garcia. Maybe he picked the better waves, though I must say I thought I was getting underscored. I was getting 7's and Sunny was getting 8's. I disputed it, and went and saw the judges later, but they said Sunny had the best of the sets, bigger and stuff, so I accepted it. But then, I was on my way.

So it was back up to Sydney for the Coke Classic at Manly. I didn't do too much. I placed 33rd to Kalani Robb. I wasn't happy. Oh well.

From there I went to Teahupoo. They had some big waves for the first couple of days of trials and the first couple of rounds of the main event. I remember beating Victor Ribas to get through the big day. Victor pretty much charges these days, so it was a big heat, but it wasn't like having a real charger. I did what needed to be done, and I remember that Victor and some of the other Brazilians complained. They reckoned that I wasn't charging as hard as Victor. My response was, 'Are you kidding me!' We really hadn't had any big sets in our heat anyway.

The next day it was pretty much perfect at 4–6'. I won, and Luke made it to the quarters before caddying for me. I was really emotional after winning. I had C. J. Hobgood in the final, and I remember paddling back out, really tired, because we had to surf four times that day. C. J. got a wave and fell near me, which meant we had a paddle race back to the take-off zone to get priority. I was just in front of C. J., and Luke was yelling and screaming to me, 'Paddle! Paddle!', pushing me. It was like it was all happening in slow-motion, like when you're in bed having a dream and you're trying to run away from someone but you can't run. I couldn't paddle. Somehow, though, I got back out there in front and won the final just as a rain squall started pouring down.

Tahiti is an incredibly beautiful and enchanting place, and I had a spiritual experience later in the day as I walked back along the back of the beach through the trees, which seemed like they were bending over me, like an archway, curtained over. At the end of the archway, there was this beautiful sunset, the glare and orange hues of light somehow forming what looked like a kind of door. I know it sounds weird, but as I stepped through it I just knew I was going to win the world title. It was like 'my' door opening—*something* had opened for me, and I was on my path to winning. It gave me the ultimate confidence.

The following week, we found ourselves up in Japan for the Marui Pro. I was hanging out with Luke Egan and shaper Darren Handley. The waves were really, really small. It was so uninteresting that we were going down to the local bar every afternoon, and we never normally do that, especially that early in the year. We were only at the fifth of 13 scheduled events. I won my first-round heat in onshore three-foot waves, but then the swell was gone for the rest of the event. I then surfed against Richie Lovett in waves that were barely a foot high. I think I just got a couple more bounces than him. It was so small we shouldn't have even been having the contest. Then I surfed my fish 'board against Rob Machado. Rob just rips those small-sized waves, but I nearly came back and got him. It was close. I got a lift with Todd Prestage and Yoshi, the O&E guy from Japan, to the airport. I was bummed I'd only got a ninth, but Todd reassured me with the fact that Kelly Slater, in previously winning world titles, had used ninths in his final result tally. They were good words to hear.

Tracing a weird course all over the South Pacific, we then went to Fiji and I won the Quiksilver Pro at Cloudbreak in rather small waves. It was mostly 3–5'. Luke, Matt Hoy and I were staying together on Namotu in Burre 1, which is Fijian for 'hut one', and one it was! We're great pals and were all stoked to be together, and I'm sure that being on a high, having that strong bond of friendship, had a lot to do with me winning. That win put me into the lead on the ratings. It seemed I was finally on track.

South Africa was next. I headed down to Jeffreys Bay feeling very confident because I absolutely love that wave. We had a bit of swell at the start. I felt really nervous though before my round-one heat. My wife Bea had given me these weird vitamin pills. I forget what they were for, but just before I was about to go out for my heat I had the hugest bowel movement and had to run back and go to the toilet. Then I got suited up again, put on my singlet, and then I had to go again. I was just freaking, thinking, 'Is this what's going to happen to me now that I'm leading the world ratings?' Somehow, I ended up having a really good heat in five-foot waves with Matt Hoy and South African Sean Holmes. Hoyo surfed good too, but I had a smoker. I ended up getting a day off while the losers surfed round two.

I was drawn against Sean Holmes again in my third-round heat, and the crowd and announcers were really pumping him up. The waves were very average. I was continually trying to out-jockey him for the inside. At one stage, after one of his waves, he got out and ran up the point, right around to Boneyards at the top of the point, and jumped back in. By the time he got towards me, a good decent-sized wave came through and he got a good score on it. Nothing much else came for me. Just like my bad run of luck on the Gold Coast, Jeffreys Bay is a contest I wanted to win so badly, but once again I'd been knocked out.

Hoyo, Bea and I then bailed town and flew up to Durban.

introduction

I don't know why I wanted to go to Durban and do a WQS event. I guess I just wanted to fill in time before flying off to America for the Huntington event a week later. I got bored there real quick. In my heat, Narrabeen's Chris Davidson got me on an interference. He even said to me, 'What are you doing here anyway?' I guess he thought that since I was leading the world WCT ratings, I somehow didn't have the right to be contesting a qualifying event. I wanted to smack him, but I didn't. That night we had a pretty big night, as so often happens in Durban. I woke up the next morning saying to myself, 'Shit man, I'm out of here!' I didn't need that. My super-good travel agent, Deby from Taylor Made in Sydney, re-routed my ticket and I flew out of

Johannesburg that night to sneak in a few days at home before flying back out for California.

I was in good spirits when I arrived in Huntington Beach. I didn't win my first-round heat, but I felt like I was surfing good. I had young Brazilian Neco Padaratz in the second round, and he kind of smoked me. I got a 33rd and I was sort of freaking, knowing that my lead was dwindling.

The next contest was Lacanau in France. Bea and I teamed up with Shane Powell, who has a standing booking for an apartment overlooking the contest site. We stayed there for a long time. Way back in 1984 I won the contest there, which was my first overseas 'A'-grade victory, so I always feel at home at Lacanau.

I'd received a great board from my shaper Rodney Dahlberg while I was home, and so everything was good. We started with big waves but then the swell dropped off. However, I still managed to surf well throughout and won all my heats, eventually making it to the final. I came second to American Tim Curran, which meant I'd slipped another counting result into my world title campaign. I was really amped.

The waves were really small at the next event at Hossegor, which is two hours south down the freeway from Lacanau, and we had to use a back-up venue a few kilometres up the beach from the usual site. I lost early, but I tried to talk myself out of being stressed about it because my averages were good. At the end of the year they only took your best eight results from your total tally of 13.

I was doing well and having fun the following week in the waves at Anglet for the opening rounds of the Billabong Pro Anglet/Mundaka. I just love the beach break there. I was on fire, until I broke my favourite board in an early round against French grommet Micky Picon. I was devastated. Good boards are just essential to success. My back-up board went pretty good though, and I made it through to the quarters. On the promise of a good and rising swell, the quarter-finals were moved to Mundaka, a fantastic, fast and furious left-hander down in the Basque country of Spain, two hours from the French border. I drove down there the afternoon before and hired a motel room. Initially, though, we were wondering what we were doing there. It was dead flat.

I woke up in the morning, when it was still dark, to this rumbling sound. It was 6–8', just perfect, and I was just *so* stoked! I was up against Taj Burrow in my quarter-final. I had a really nice comfortable exchange, stalling into tubes, putting my arm into the wall to slow down under the pitching lip and virtually just getting tubed at will. I'm a goofy-footer, so I was on my forehand. Taj was on his backhand, and it's hard to master that wave with your back to it. I won the heat easily, and I remember that Taj left feeling pretty upset because he was coming second in the ratings at the time. It had been his big chance to beat me and narrow the gap.

In the semi-final I had Mark Bannister. He got one pretty good barrel, but other than that I was pretty much in control. In the final it was me versus Guilherme Herdy, and he started trying to do floaters; that's something you just *don't* do at Mundaka. I had a good final and won, and was absolutely ecstatic. I was so happy. I was with Bea and Craig Sage, an Aussie expatriate who lives there and is Spain Billabong rep, along with Inigo and Marianne Letamendia, who are close friends and own Pukas, the biggest and best surf shop chain in the Basque country. We partied on for days. It was the ultimate celebration, so we left feeling somewhat worse for wear when we drove back to France, packed our bags and flew home.

I had a great five weeks at home, and didn't think much about surfing at all. I played a lot of golf and kept up the training, but there wasn't a lot of waves. I didn't want to let the lead get to me, so I was pretty relaxed when we flew off to Rio de Janeiro in Brazil. I'd had heaps of headlines, media and press when I'd got home from France, but I still didn't think winning the world title was going to be an issue before we got to Hawaii, which is a few weeks after the Brazilian leg. I still found it hard to believe that I could possibly win the world title, but I was just so stoked to even be in the position where I *could* win. It just seemed like a dream.

Fernando Rego from Oakley picked me up from the airport in Rio. He's a great mate from way back. We had a few beers together, as is a tradition on my first night back in Brazil. The next day the contest hadn't started and I remember feeling really lonely. My golf mate Bone was there, but he'd had a huge one the previous night and was just out cold. Bea hadn't come on that leg of the tour, and those dingy apartment rooms had no TV or anything — well, they were gabbling Portuguese anyway. Just as I was thinking how dark and lonely it was, the phone rang, and it was Luke Egan, apologising that he hadn't been able to find anywhere to stay and wondering if he could 'impose' and move in with me. 'Unreal! Get over here!' I almost yelled through the phone. I was stoked. I helped him up with his bags, and we went out to dinner at the local *rodizio*, which are these incredible meat smorgasboard restaurants they have in Brazil. You pay a set fee and heaps of waiters just walk around, table to table, offering you every sort of meat you could ever imagine. It's unreal.

I woke up the next morning stoked. Bone had returned to the land of the living, and was cooking us bacon and eggs for breakfast, and so there I was, with two of my best mates, thinking, 'Wow! Life aint so bad after all! You're leading the ratings, and if you do real good here you could win the world title right here this week!' In my first-round heat I had local grommet Railo Monteiro. He ripped, but I must say I felt I was hard done by on one exchange. Monteiro did two big turns on one wave and got a 7.5, but then I got a three-foot double up which I just fully went to town on, and the judges only gave me a 6.5; I really felt it was worth a 9.0. I went up to the tower and complained, but head judge Perry Hatchett told me that I shouldn't complain. 'Bullshit!' I protested. Losing three points is a rather big and intolerable shortfall.

In round two I had another Brazilian, and I had a nice calm heat. I showed no nerves and felt pleased with myself. Back up in our rented apartment, I was getting along well with Luke and Bone, and everything was great. The next day, however, had a bit of a messy start to it. I got up and had my morning constitutional but then discovered, to my horror, that we were out of toilet paper and we had no newspaper, magazines or anything that could substitute for it. I guess I should have just jumped in the shower, but instead, in a hurry to get down to the surf before the contest was scheduled to start, I just jumped in my wetsuit, reasoning that the surf could do the job. I don't know that I should even be relating this, but anyway … you couldn't see the surf from our apartment, so I've just rocked down to the beach, only to find it's basically dead flat. I had to go out anyway, for obvious reasons. Everyone was looking at me, just going, 'What is he doing?' In hindsight, despite being in a bit of a panic at the time, it was pretty funny.

So the sky was dark and gloomy, and the waves were real tiny and the organisers didn't know whether to start or not. While they were debating the issue, I remember sitting down with Noodles Webster, Taj Burrow and Todd Prestage, who shared a hilarious story with me. The boys on tour have always got classic tales to tell. Sharing the highs and lows of being on the road is one of the things that makes us all so tight. The contest got postponed for a noon call and, blow me down, while we waited the swell started picking up.

They moved the contest down the beach to a bank that was serving the swell up better, and we were on. It was round three, and I was drawn in heat eight against that Monteiro kid again. A really big crowd was starting to build on the beach too. The Brazilians are a bit like the Europeans when it comes to getting out of bed — the later the better. They usually don't get to the beach until after lunch. Before my heat, some of the people that were around me in the ratings started losing their exchanges. But Taj, one of the main guys who could catch me, survived his heat.

I paddled out, not thinking anything of the ratings situation. At the same time, I must admit I was a bit concerned about Monteiro, because he was a good surfer, though he was riding a different board from the one he used in our other heat. He looked strong when the waves were bigger, but in the smaller stuff he wasn't as threatening. He was looking a little slow. I had a good heat. I was weaving some good turns, and milking the waves as best I could, only getting sixes but still staying in control of the heat. At the end of it, I think my young foe needed almost a combination score or combo, which is two waves, to catch me. As the hooter sounded I was happy, thinking to myself, 'Yes, I've got at least a ninth — another step closer.'

When I got to the beach, there were more cameras than usual focused on me, like four or five TV cameras. I remember looking at them and thinking it was a bit strange. Next thing Monteiro, in a nice gesture, stepped up to me and shook my hand, but then didn't let go and lifted my arm up, like 'No. 1!'. I was getting rather confused. By then all the TV cameras were crowding around and in my face in a big frenzy.

One of the journalists said, 'Hey Mark, do you realise that if Mick Campbell doesn't win this next heat, you will have won the world title?'

I had no idea. All I could say was, 'You are kidding me, aren't you?'

'No, no Mark. I'm not kidding you!'

I just instantly broke away from the media pack and sprinted up the beach. My head was absolutely spinning. Then I flashed that I didn't even know where Mick was out there at that moment, or who he was surfing against. I turned back around to the line-up and the first thing I saw was Flavio Padaratz absolutely ripping up a wave. Knowing he'd just got a big score, I just thought, 'No way!' I continued running up the beach, got changed and then saw Luke. 'You know what's going on, don't you?' he asked with raised eyebrows. I couldn't talk. I ran along the promenade a bit and had a coconut juice from one of the little stands that dot the back of the beach at Barra. I even felt like asking them to put straight vodka in it. I ended up having a sly little beer. I had to settle down. My heart was just racing.

Then I went back to trying to watch the heat. Bone was with me, and all these people were just gathering around, like bees around a honeypot. Security crew were trying to keep them away, but without much effect. Through the crowd I could see that Flavio was pretty much waxing Mick, and I was like, 'No way! No! No! It's gonna happen right now, you're kidding me!' I just started jumping up and down. 'Now! Right now, it's going to happen now!' Things were getting out of hand and the security guys dragged me back to the event tower. They counted down the heat, and I counted it down, and that was it — I was *world champion*! Far out! The rest is history. That night I booked out the whole of the local Mexican restaurant and every Aussie on tour came out to dinner, all the chick surfers, all my mates. It was great. A big one!

The deal was done, but on we went to Pipeline in Hawaii. I didn't have a very good Triple Crown. I lost early at Haleiwa, and at Sunset too. Sunset got big and good, and the best thing was that young Aussie Zane Harrison stepped up to the plate and surfed unreal and won the contest. By doing that he got into the trials for Pipeline, and charged through them in 10–12' waves to make the main event. I drew him in ten-foot waves. The kid was obviously on fire, but I had a good heat too, getting eight points on one big wave, and made it through. It was a real good feeling because I'd already won the title, and previously I've seen people win the title and not carry through at Pipe. Pipe is one of my favourite spots, and beating Zane out there in big pushy waves was really putting another little feather in my cap.

I ended up making it all the way to the semi-finals, where I came up against Kelly Slater. I had him too — in the bag and stitched up. I was sitting out there towards the end of the heat and was so relaxed that I started playing with my fingernails. I was bored. I had him comboed. Kelly was splashing water around in frustration, but then they gave him a pretty high score of 5.0 for a little left. Admittedly, I didn't see it, but that let him back in it, and then he needed a high eight or a nine — an 8.75, I think.

With about a minute to go, a little four-foot wave came, and I guess I wasn't concentrating. I looked at him instead of the wave, and there was no way he was going to get an 8.75 on that wave. But he paddled into it like he was going to get it. Having priority, I just instinctively took the wave, obviously without thinking properly. I blundered! There were like 45 seconds left and I was just cursing myself, going, 'You idiot! You've got one chance. If there's a wave after this, he can beat you.' I paddled over a wave and there it was, one of the best waves of the day. He paddled into it just laughing, pulled into a big backdoor barrel and got a 10. I just put my head down and said, 'Well, you can't have everything.'

In the wash-up, though, I extended my lead at Pipe, so I was stoked. Best of all, I had done it at last! I was the world champion!

january›february 2000

February
January

jan › feb 2000

THE NEW CENTURY STARTED for me with a party, presumably just like everyone else in the world. I'd just returned home from Hawaii two or three days earlier. We started the festivities mid afternoon on New Year's Eve with a barbecue at my house. About 50 people rocked up, and it was a really diverse collection of people.

I had a few mates up from Sydney, including one of my old mates from my hometown of Kurnell. Let's get it straight right from the start. Everyone says I'm from Cronulla, but they're wrong. Right next to it is a place so small they call it a 'village'. This village is called Kurnell. The major landmark is a big ugly industrial monster called 'AOR', which stands for Australian Oil Refinery. Around the AOR is a bunch of houses, maybe a couple of hundred of them. They say that if the AOR ever blew, it'd take out most of the Sutherland Shire, and everything within a 10-kilometre radius thereafter. That's one hell of a bang. But in the meantime, Kurnell is one of the quietest places in Sydney. It's a million miles from caring.

Captain Cook, in 1770, set foot on Aussie soil not less than 300 metres from where I was raised. The Occhilupo family household, in fact, is the closest to Australia's so-called 'landing place', where Captain Cook first set foot on our turf and claimed it for Mother England. So that's where I am from. Admittedly I do digress but this important point has to be clarified.

So, anyway, one of my Kurnell mates was up for New Year's Eve. His name is Brett Schweickle, but we all call him 'Beaver'. I grew up in Kurnell with Beaver, Richard Maurer, the Darcy brothers Stuart and Dave, and two other mates that I rarely see these days, Stuart Collins and Robert Potter. That was our gang. Luke Egan was there at the barbie too, along with Darren Handley, a lot of Bea's friends, and all my golfing mates. It was a really good barbie to see in the new century. Everyone drank so much beer. By 6 pm I was severely under the influence. I was smashed, just as you would expect to be on the last day of the twentieth century.

Later on that night we were off to Darren Handley's party, and after that to Brenden 'Margo' Margieson's party. Margo was having a fancy-dress party, like a lot of people that night, but I got a bit too prepared for it. I didn't know what to wear, so I went into Bea's closet and grabbed one of her summer frocks. That was it — nothing except for a frock and a scarf round my head. No lippie, no stuffed artificial boobs, no nothing, I just looked really weird. I had three pairs of underpants stuffed below, it was that tight a frock. You know, I had to keep my big thing down (ha, ha)! So we got to DH's, and it wasn't fancy-dress, but there I was wearing a dress. Everyone thought I was off the planet, which I was. I saw the photos from the night, and I was downright ugly. Until I saw the photos I was wondering why no one wanted to hang around with me that night. But when I saw them I knew. Then we rocked up to Margo's, and Joel Parkinson had hooked

up with us by then. At the end of the night, Joel was really pissed and was getting really obnoxious, calling me a transvestite and stuff. Once again, I understood where he was coming from when I saw the photos.

We were back at Luke's sitting next to an open fire in the backyard when the sun came up on New Year's Day, but Joel was still calling me a transvestite. I was going to smash him, but after I saw the photos I thought, 'Strewth, he was right to call me that.' I really did look that bad. But Joel will pay eventually. Anyway, we were intending to kick on all day, but of course it didn't happen. We'd done well to see in the dawn, however I soon hit the sack like a runaway train.

Surprisingly, it didn't take me any time to recover. That

afternoon I went down to Seagulls, my local club, via a couple of hamburgers from the top shop. I had a few beers and it was all over. The party was over. Thereafter I got pretty much stuck straight into training and turned all serious. My major focus became getting really fit.

The following couple of months were really busy. I did a lot of promos. I went down to Sydney to work on my CD and had to do like 50 interviews in one day, just sitting on the phone, sitting in my hotel room at Star City. Sitting and talking. I also did promos for Warner Bros in their studios for the *Roccymentary* CD. It was kind of frustrating because everyone kept asking me questions about surfing, but all I wanted anyone to ask me was how good a singer did I think I was. Later, I went on Molly Meldrum's former show, *House of Hits*. I had to walk up this catwalk in front of a live studio audience to reach the main set for my interview. I also met singer Deni Hines that night. She was a really friendly character. Working with Molly and appearing on the show was really good fun. It was about the fourth or so time I'd met Molly. We're good friends now, but not *that* good if you know what I mean!

What else did I do? I went down to Melbourne with Geoff Rafter and we met Pat and his family. Pat was training down there while the Australian Open was on, but he was really frustrated because he had a bung shoulder and couldn't compete. We got tickets to the tennis and watched Andre Agassi up against Pete Sampras; it was great, something completely different. It was the first time I'd ever watched a tennis match. Later, I met all the crew. Pat took us out to a tennis party at a nightclub and we met Gustavo Kuerten, the Brazilian, who surfs too. He was really cool, as was Pat, as always. Pat also took us out to dinner one night with his girlfriend

Lara. Actually it was me, Pat, Lara and my golfing mate from home, Bone. A kind of strange scenario ensued. We were sitting at the table and there was no Mrs Rafter. Like all women, Lara takes a bit of time to 'get ready'. She eventually came down to the restaurant, from their room upstairs. Naturally, I got up to move along from sitting next to Pat, but Pat said, 'No, don't you move, she's the one that's taken forever, you sit next to me, I want to talk to you.' So Lara sat on the other side of me. She was cool though. She used to be in the surfing industry a bit and she's a really nice girl; they're a great couple. After dinner, Pat took us out to this nightclub, and it was really funny. I was hanging out with ... what's that chick's name? The blonde one. Anna Kournikova.

The following day we went down to Bells and met up with Damien Oliver, the jockey. It was our first meeting. We took him down to Bird Rock, and had a great little surf and then Damien had to bail and catch a plane to Sydney to race at Rosehill. While we were down in Victoria a really big party was put on by Globe Shoes, my shoe sponsor. While we were doing the tapes for this book, Sarge interrupted me and asked whether it was hard for me to adapt to wearing shoes. I never ever used to wear shoes, but then I got sponsored by a shoe company. Sarge asked me if it was a 'mission' to get used to wearing shoes, and I instantly replied, "No, it was a mis-shoe."' Sarge just broke up. I dunno. Sometimes, actually often, things come out of my mouth that I don't think about; they just come, and everyone around me just cracks up. I don't mean to be a comedian, in fact it's the last thing I'd like to be, but it's good to lead people to laughter.

Taj Burrow was in Melbourne at the same time, and we hung out together. One night we went to a party, near the Globe factory, then eventually we made it to the Globe factory party with shaper Maurice Cole and his wife Anne, and Geoff Rafter. At the party they had a big halfpipe, and juggling acts — all kinds of stuff. They had so much happening. Another night, Taj and I had to go to another barbie they had down at Bells, at Stephen Hill's house. At about 11 pm, they blew up about 50 Globe footballs and decided that Taj and I had to sign all the footballs for everyone in the joint. At 11 pm at night, it really was a mission. A late promo that one.

While all this was going on I was trying to train, but every time I got a roll going, I was interrupted by duties to either Billabong, Oakley, Globe or Warner Bros. Such is the price of being a World Champion. In that first two months of the year, I had to *give* away

something like 50 surfboards for promos, auctions, charities — you name it, people just wanted a piece of me *and* my boards. The amount of promos I did in that two months was just unbelievable. I could never have imagined how demanding being a World Champion really is. Just on the surfboard count, if only I'd known how many I'd have to give away I'd have had Rodney Dahlberg shape 50 boards just for the purpose. Instead, I had to give away boards that meant something to me.

So every time I got a week or two under my belt at home, I had to leave town for a promo. It was really distracting, but at the same time I knew it went with the territory. The best thing that happened in that two months was that, towards the end of it, Kirra pumped for about 10 days. It was stormy, but there were plenty of clean 6–8' sections, and sometimes full runners down the length of the point. Because it was stormy, there weren't that many people regularly out there. Those of us that got out there, day after day, were fully rewarded. We were doing the runaround all day long, a minimum of three hours a session. It was the best form of training you could ever have. You just don't get bored. When you're running around the point, you're looking out over someone getting barrelled, or someone ripping into a section, and then you get to paddle out again and have a go yourself, amped by what you've just seen. That's the way it is in the surf every session. Everyone is out to better everything that is going on around them. Paddling out off the corner of Coolangatta Beach, you do a sprint paddle out to give yourself enough space between you and the big groyne because of the current that draws you to it. Then, as soon as you get out, you basically have to catch a wave because you can't stay where you want to because of the rip.

It sucks you down the point. It's hectic, but it's unreal. It's a severe workout.

About a week before the Billabong Pro was due to start, the ocean went flat. I'd had a great few weeks of swell though, so I wasn't complaining. I'd had heaps of good surfs with my stepson Rainer, and Robbie Page was up at the time too, staying at Sarge's place, and out there for many of the sessions at Kirra. Robbie and I spent our grommethood at Black Rock together trying to outdo Terry Richardson. Those were the days. Nick Wood was out there at Kirra every morning. He's a Kirraholic. I'm an early riser, but when we're paddling out at first light, he's already paddling in, session completed. He's such a good surfer, such a good man, and so, so keen. I played only a little golf over that period. Beyond snowboarding, golf is my alternate passion but I didn't have a lot of time to indulge in it during this period. I missed it. By my recollection, it was a rather crazy, mixed-up two months of total unpredictability. Such is life.

march 2000

March

WEDNESDAY 1 ›››› MONDAY 6

THOUGH I'D ALREADY BEEN doing a lot of training, and certainly lots of mental preparation, the real work began on 1 March. With the opening World Championship Tour (WCT) event of the season, the Billabong Pro, scheduled to start on 9 March, it was time for serious physical tuning and narrowing of focus. Every other morning through most of February, I'd been getting up early, as I always do, literally with the birds, and putting in some hard yards down on the back beach at Fingal Head.

Fingal is a real special place. It's right on the NSW–Queensland border, just across the Tweed River from Tweed Heads, Coolangatta, and one of the most consistent wave locations, certainly one of my favourite surfing places, Duranbah. I love Fingal so much. I did most of my training there for my successful world title comeback attempt.

Fingal's back beach is totally uninhabited. Usually there are only a few joggers, some fishermen and a handful of surfers along the entire four kilometres of beach which stretches south down to Kingscliff. The place has a real aura, and is all Aboriginal land.

I actually bought a property there at the start of the year, but sometimes I feel awkward about it. At times, I feel I should give my land back to the local Aboriginals. There are a lot of Aboriginals living on the other side of the headland, behind the two kilometres of beach that extends up to the southern groyne on the Tweed River mouth. It's a beautiful place, and I've always liked it. Like many surfers, I often go there during the day when the wind is north-east, because the waves are protected there behind the headland. The waves aren't all-time, but they're really fun.

So every morning I'd been running about five or six kilometres, poking a stick in the soft sand and moving it further and further up the beach with every following day. Even at an early hour, the sun has a lot of heat in it on the Gold Coast, and most mornings on that nine-day stretch were clear with beautiful sunrises, so I'd get really hot and sweaty as I ran, which I like; I could feel myself getting really fit. Running along, I would think about the year ahead, not unlike what I did the previous year in my build-up to winning the world title. A lot of training in the 1999 pre-season had got me through the year. It's a real grind at the start of the season, a shock to the system, because you go from the Billabong, then to Bells and then to Tahiti and Fiji in fairly quick succession.

Needless to say, at the time I was surfing a lot too, and I felt that I was in good form. I tried a lot of different boards in that period but, in hindsight, I think it was a mistake. I should have just stayed on the equipment that my regular shaper Rodney Dahlberg was producing for me — really nice channel bottoms. It was naive of me to think I could find something better.

I played a little golf in the lead-up to the Billabong as well. I had my best round at The Meadows at Broadbeach. I played with my old mate Steve Harmston, who used to manage the Mount Woodgee surf shop. He's a pretty good golfer, but not that good, and I can take his money. I love the guy — we play for big dollars, and he rarely beats me. I've got my handicap down from 27 to 19 over the past two years, but I've never been able to crack the eighties. At The Meadows, I nearly made it. I blew it by missing a few short putts. All up, though, I reckon my golf is going good. For me, if my golf is going good, everything else is going good. Golf's a tough game — it's even harder than surfing! When you're stressed some times, you just can't hit the ball straight. Anyway, as soon as the Billabong Pro started, that was it for me … no more golf!

All the way through the contest build-up, I was tied up with heaps of promotions for Billabong and press interviews and stuff. I seemed to be averaging at least two promos a day. At one stage, I commented to Sarge that I should change my name to Mark 'Promo' Occhilupo. Sarge broke into hysterics, but seriously, it's true! I had to do a ton of promos for the *Roccymentary* music compilation too. I didn't like the workload, but was obviously pretty much obligated to do it. Besides that, I've always had a problem saying no. All I want to do is train and surf, but all the other stuff makes it difficult. Sometimes, it just turns my lifestyle into more of a job than a love or passion, but I guess it's not all that bad!

Becoming world champion has changed my life a lot, but it's mostly been for the better. It's focused more attention onto me, and on my story, everything. Sure, it's meant a fair amount of extra money has come in, but along with that comes lots of haggling. It just all happened all of a sudden, but I wanted it to happen. It was like a destiny thing. There was a lot of luck involved, of course, but I *tried* to make it happen. You can't always turn the pages yourself, though.

The whole process has obviously forced me to mature a lot. The sport of surfing has given me a lot, and it's my duty to put something back into it, even if it encroaches on my space. As reigning world champion, I'm sort of a roving ambassador for the sport, and that's definitely a weight on my shoulders.

Speaking of world champions, there was a lot of hype leading up to the start of the Billabong Pro about Kelly Slater, who was a wildcard for the event. A lot of people were freaking to me about how unfair it was that he, now unrated, would be the lowest seed, and that because I was the highest seed, we'd meet in the first round. I wasn't really worried about it, though. I was actually surprised that he wanted to come to the event.

On the other hand, I wasn't surprised that Billabong wanted him in, because he's such a drawcard for the media and crowds. Last year he came and left, and didn't even surf his third-round heat. He wasn't into it at all. He's not much into competing at the moment. He'd rather just cruise around and just *be* Kelly. Yeah, anyway, so they were all ringing me, saying Kelly was the wildcard, but I was just going, 'Yeah, well I'll believe it when I see it,' and I was right. He didn't come. I knew it was going to happen.

TUESDAY 7

As the final countdown for the contest kick-off crept up on us, we helped our pommy mate, Russell Winter, settle in. He and his girlfriend Jackie arrived a few days earlier and moved in next door to our apartment at Kirra. Jackie is a good friend of my wife Beatrice (Bea), and since they hang around a lot together,

Russell and I were doing likewise. I took him for a surf down at Fingal on the first morning of the Billabong Pro waiting-period. While I went for a run he caught a few waves, even though they were really small. I must confess I don't particularly like Russell's style, but he is a good surfer and goes for the big moves. When he's on, he's pretty damn good. I love the fact that he's the only European surfer to make the top 44 tour. It's a real accomplishment. I've been going to England since I was really young, and the surfers coming through the ranks don't have a lot of talent over there to bounce off and progress with, so Russ has done really well to get where he has. We played a bit of golf that afternoon too. Russ is still learning, but like his surfing, when he's on, he can really hit 'em.

WEDNESDAY 8

ALL AMPED ON THE EVE of the opening event for the season, the Billabong Pro, I was awake and up before dawn, but then was disappointed to find the waves almost flat again. After a light run along Fingal I got a bit of breakfast and headed up to Burleigh Heads for the event launch and press conference. Usually it's held in the Pavillion at Burleigh, but this year it was upstairs in the restaurant and bar area atop Burleigh Surf Club. As the camera crews set up on the balcony, we looked straight up the point. It was barely breaking.

It was a cruisy press conference. After all, it was on the Gold Coast, my home. I knew almost all the people in the room. There's a surf-centred culture on the coast, probably one of the few places in the world where there's surfing on the TV news most nights. I see most of the cameramen or journos around the traps, checking the surf, whatever. They often shoot you having an early surf for *Surfwatch*, for almost all the TV channels, or for weather segments. At the press conference, there were all the same faces looking at me, just a different scenario.

It was a funny gathering actually. I got asked some questions that I thought were pretty irrelevant. They progressively put about ten of us up to the microphone to field questions. Joel Parkinson's turn was pretty funny. He got asked what he thought was an awkward question, and didn't really handle it very well. Like, I'm not putting him down, he was trying to show his confidence and he is a confident kid (as well as an unreal surfer), but he kind of threw the question back at the TV journalist and made the poor guy a laughing stock. The media also asked Joel whether he thought he was going to have to beat me in the contest, and he answered, 'What do you mean?' It was relevant because we could have drawn each other if we both won our first-round heats. He just didn't get it, I guess.

THURSDAY 9

THE WAVES WERE REALLY small, but I had heaps to do anyway. Earlier in the week, Bea and I had moved down from our beautiful home at Bilambil into our apartment on the headland at Kirra to be closer to the beach.

Almost single-handedly, Bea had done an amazing renovation job on the place. She'd even raised our bed two metres, on top of this beautiful cabinet, so that I didn't have to lift my head from the pillow to check the surf. After new paint, carpet, furniture, blinds, almost everything, and on a sensible budget, the place looked really nice. Bea is an unbelievable homemaker, unsurpassed I'd say. However, despite the fact that I stayed there for two days, it just didn't feel like I was at home. We didn't have cable TV either. We wanted to get cable put on, but we were going to have to buy it for the whole block of units. Our home at Bilambil is my sanctuary. It's gorgeous, and I love it. I said to Bea, 'Honey, it feels like I'm away and I'm only ten minutes from home. I want to go home.' After all the work she'd done on the place, Bea was understandably less than impressed, but she relented and we moved back to our real home, our castle. We then moved Jackie and Russell into our apartment, so they were styling in a basically new pad. Rent-free too. They were stoked.

That night, with most of the top 44 crew, I went to the Surfers' Meeting in a convention room adjacent to ASP International's new offices at Coolangatta. Our new headquarters are incredible; fully sponsored by the Queensland Government, they would do any international organisation proud. They have these surfers' meetings fairly regularly, every few events, but I don't usually go because I'm usually psyching for the contest, and like to go to bed really early too. I went to this one though, and it was interesting. I sat between Luke Egan and Beau Emerton, around a massive conference table with everyone else. We had a few beers and had a good time while the meeting rolled on. We always manage to have a good time one way or another.

At the end of the meeting, it was my honour to make a special presentation to our mate, Greville Mitchell. Grev is an English gentleman, a philanthropist — a what? Yeah, that's what I said.

A philanthropist is someone who generously supports worthy causes out of the goodness of his/her heart. Well, thank God, Grev, who is an experienced and accomplished corporate businessman, has taken a big interest in pro surfing, and more to the point, the surfers themselves. More than anyone, he cares about the surfers. We have actually elected him as a surfers' representative on the ASP Board, and that shows how much we love him and trust him. Anyway, as a gesture of thanks for all that he has done for us, the entire top 44 signed the surfboard that I won the Billabong Pro on last year at Anglet/Mundaka in the Basque country of northern Spain. I presented it to him on behalf of all the boys, and he was just *so* stoked. It was great to see. He and his family are really special.

SATURDAY 11

AFTER WAITING FOR SWELL for two days, we finally got some action in the ocean on the Saturday, and especially being the weekend, Burleigh headland was packed with people watching. The surf wasn't that good, but way better than what we'd been having. I had a drama before I even got in the water for my heat — my board was locked in my car!

Russell had been hanging out and cruising in my car, and as my heat approached, I told him that I was taking my spare board down to the competitor's area, and that I'd be back. I guess he wasn't listening, because when I got back to the car he was gone, with my car keys, and the board I wanted to ride in my heat was locked inside. It later transpired that he gone for lunch down in the main street of Burleigh Heads. I wasn't very happy. I had him paged by the announcers, and then everyone knew of my dilemma, which was very embarrassing.

When I got back to my car there were people gathered all around it, including TV cameramen. Local lensman Gordo had his camera in my face, and I was telling him to get it away. He's such a light-hearted comedian, Gordo, that he didn't get the message and I just had to handle it. All these kids were saying, 'Break the glass! Break the glass!' but I thought, 'No way!' I'd surf my spare board before breaking the glass of my beloved Jeep. As it turned out, I should have ridden that 'spare' board — a thicker board with six deep channels. In the meantime, some kind guy

who had heard the announcement for Russell and had recalled seeing him down the street, ran down to Burleigh to get my keys, and sprinted back with them in about five minutes. I really appreciated that. Thanks mate, whoever you are. So I finally got into my car, got the board I wanted, ran for my heat, and was out there in the water with just a minute remaining.

It was a bad way to kick off the contest. I was flustered, and for me that's just the worst way to be. The only time I can't surf like I should is when I'm flustered. I just try too much, too quick, too hard. My first turn on my first wave felt really good, but from then on I just couldn't find the right spot on the board. I just kept pushing it way too hard, and not surfing it properly. Everyone has a different stance on a board, but generally you have one foot in a spot over the fins, and another three-quarters up the board. Some boards are really good, and you can move your feet one or two inches around that certain sweet spot and still be OK, but then on other boards, if you don't have your feet in exactly the right spot, the board just won't go. I thought the board I was riding, shaped by Darren Handley, was a magic one, but my very first surf on it felt weird, even though I had had some really good surfs on it. In that heat, though, it didn't feel too good. No matter what, I just couldn't seem to find that sweet spot. Being flustered, I was thinking way too much. The heat just ran away from me. It's really easy to beat *yourself* in a heat, and that's basically what I did. After that reasonable enough start, I had a bit of an ongoing distraction with Shaun Cansdell trying to hassle me and paddle me up the point. It's frustrating, but sometimes wildcards, particularly aspiring grommets, can be a bit amped or overkeen, and you get hassled out. Among the top 44 we don't usually hassle at all in the first-round three-man heats. I was still within range of the heat but then Kalani Robb, who had free rein on wave selection because of our paddling games, ended up getting a late wave and nailing the result.

I got a good surf in that morning before the contest, but other than that, I hadn't really surfed Burleigh much when it had been good. I think I'd been up there and surfed only once, a few weeks earlier when it was about 4–5', but the sandbanks were really bad, really straight, and so it wasn't anywhere near as good as Burleigh gets. It was a quick, peaky wave, and so even though I'd originally intended to go up there more often to train, it hadn't worked out that way.

I love Burleigh, and I've had some unreal sessions out there over the years, but it's a good 30-minute drive up into Queensland. That might sound a bit strange, but even though I live on the Gold Coast, I actually live just south of the border at Bilambil. Coming originally from Kurnell, near Cronulla on Sydney's southern beaches, I'm a NSW boy at heart. I love it up in Queensland, but my favourite beach, which I try to surf as much as possible, is still Duranbah in NSW. When the swell is up, I surf Kirra. I adore Kirra, so that's why I don't go to Burleigh much when it's good. I know it's one of the best waves in the world, but it doesn't do anything for me. As long as the swell is big enough, Kirra is going to be working as well as Burleigh is at the same time, so Kirra is where I prefer to surf.

SUNDAY 12

Up and amped at first light I was bummed to drive down to Snapper and find that the swell had dropped right off. Sometimes I get really frustrated with those wave prediction people and meteorologists. The previous day's swell was not supposed to die like that. Oh, what am I saying? Obviously nobody can really tell what the weather and waves are going to do. The ocean is a blessing, but also a source of frustration sometimes. They ended up postponing the men's competition and having the women's event. I cruised around late morning looking for waves, but then spent most of the rest of the day cruising back up at home, hoping for waves tomorrow.

MONDAY 13

I FELL ASLEEP EXTRA early the previous night, and woke up about 4.30 am. It's such a nice time to wake up; everything is so peaceful and quiet, especially up at Bilambil. I don't know where kookaburras sleep, and I don't know if it's always the same one, but every morning, at the crack of dawn, one starts laughing, sometimes with a couple of other birds. I know their noises, and as soon as I hear them, I know it's morning. They wake me up, and sometimes I wake them up too. That probably sounds odd, but sometimes, I swear, if I wake up a bit earlier than them they're like, 'No way! He beat us!'

It's not just the sounds that make Bilambil so special, but the sights as well. It is such a gorgeous area, with amazing natural colours everywhere. It seems to rain at some point every day, so it's really green. Our house is about 800 metres above sea level, so if there's a wisp of cloud around, or the Goldy is due for an afternoon storm and it's even looking remotely like rain, we'll get it. That makes the air up there on the mountain range extra clean too.

I headed down to Snapper Rocks at about ten to five, thinking the contest might be on there, but it wasn't very good, so I drove up to the main contest site at Burleigh Heads. There they had us on standby for hours, waiting for it to get better with the tide. Like I said, the banks weren't very good at Burleigh, so I was pretty keen not to have it there. Snapper actually had a good bank, but it didn't look so good that morning. Duranbah had a good bank, too, but it was actually losing some form. A week prior to the event it had been fine, but now it was starting to lose sand in some spots and getting a bit flat.

I'd been getting up and surfing Duranbah almost every morning for weeks. Luke Egan would ring me on my mobile and meet me up the top of the hill overlooking the beach and the Tweed River mouth. The bank was really stable for a long time, with a great channel in against the groyne. You could have a great ride, straighten out on it, and then get an elevator ride back to the take-off zone via the rip in the channel against the groyne. It was great. I thought all that time that if there wasn't much swell for the contest, it would be at Duranbah for sure, but no, it was at Snapper and Burleigh, and only at Duranbah on the last day, and I was knocked out by then.

Eventually, at about 10.45 am, they cancelled the contest for the day, and everybody scattered far and wide. Luke and I had been talking all morning about ducking off somewhere for a surf if the contest was postponed. We'd agreed to meet on the back beach at Fingal. Barton Lynch and the TV camera crew he works with for his Channel Ten surfing show, along with Sarge, were going to meet us there. When they canned the contest I jumped straight into my Jeep and headed for the Healthy Bee for my daily constitutional smoothie — soy milk, banana, papaya, lecithin and wheatgerm. I just had to stop and get one on my way to Fingal.

I also stopped at Chinderah, at the base of the Fingal Peninsula, to get some petrol. I guess I took my time because as I was driving out of the petrol station, Luke, Darren Handley and Sarge were driving south past the garage. Although we were only about 200 metres apart when they pulled over down the road, Luke phoned me on his mobile and said they'd checked Fingal and that the waves weren't too good. Barton and his crew hadn't turned up. We decided to go down the coast further. We checked several

spots, back and forth, up and down, as you do when you're doing the surf check. The tide was kind of wrong wherever we looked, but eventually we decided to go back to a left-hand inside suck on an open beach.

It was about three foot, some a little bigger, and I was fortunate enough to slip straight into a nice little barrel as I paddled out. It seemed it was going to be a good, fun surf, but the rip down the beach was really strong, and the three of us were way down the beach before we knew it. After about my third wave I discovered that one of my fins was hanging loose. It could have been like that the whole time.

On my way back to the car to get another board, I was talking to Sarge on the beach for a bit when I spotted a good barrelling left way near where we'd first paddled out, so when I went back in I tried to stay up there. Luke eventually paddled back up there, too, and we each caught a few clean, smaller ones up on that bank before I decided I should go and get my board fixed. I'd dinged, creased or dislodged fins on three boards in three sessions. It was time to go to the factory for repairs. Despite everything, it had turned out to be a good day.

TUESDAY 14

BECAUSE I'D LOST THAT three-man round-one heat, I had to surf through round two when the contest reconvened at Snapper Rocks. In WCTs, if you win your round-one heat, you go straight to round three. However, if you lose, you have to battle through round two.

Since I was the highest seed, I was drawn in the first heat of the day against the lowest seed, young Shaun Cansdell from Mullaway, near Coffs Harbour. To everyone's surprise, he didn't turn up. I guess he had presumed that the contest would be at Burleigh, and discovered too late that it had been moved to Snapper.

I've been doing the tour for 15 years — well eight years actually, taking into account the years I spent off the tour, in an 18-year career as a 'pro' surfer — and it's pretty rare for your opponent to not turn up for his heat. I can remember one time at Bells when Mike Burness didn't turn up for our quarter-final early one morning. It was six foot and quite good. He eventually turned up with five minutes to go. Another time I was drawn against Joel Fitzgerald, ironically at Snapper, and he didn't turn up until there was about eight minutes left on the clock. Even though I like to turn up for heats as late as possible, some people leave it really late, especially Kelly Slater.

I had a sneaking suspicion that Shaun wasn't going to turn up for the heat. I don't know why. So, there I was, out there in a nice 2–3' swell, by myself in the first heat of the day, just loving it — absolutely *loving* it. Well, to be honest, I wasn't really enjoying it as much as I should have been, as I was thinking that Shaun would show up any minute. I deliberately let some beautiful waves go by. On any given day, almost no matter what, there's often 50 or even 100 people out there in the surf and not a wave goes to waste. I wanted a few nice ones to go through unridden because it never really happens. Of course, one of the great things about surfing in heats is that you're out there with just one or two other people in the line-up. It's great to just let a wave roll through with no one on it.

So Shaun never made it. I saw him as I drove out of the carpark. He had his head down, and was standing next to shaper Greg Webber. I felt sorry for Shaun. It was pretty heavy for him to miss out. I saw him the next day and told him it happens to everyone, on at one time or another. He was still devastated. I'm really not 100 per cent sure, but I can't remember having missed one myself.

WEDNESDAY 15

A HEAVY DAY. I was drawn against Joel Parkinson for my third-round heat, and was real nervous. Being up against Joel is as heavy as Kelly Slater. Before the contest everyone was saying, 'Wow, you're going to have Kelly first heat,' but I wasn't worried in the slightest because I didn't think he was going to turn up anyway. And I was right — he didn't. Normally, not many

wildcards get through their first- or second-round heats, but I knew that in Joel's case it was more than likely he would and more, and I was sure I'd draw him sooner or later.

Joel is a good friend of mine, and a great kid. I admire his surfing so much. He's not just a good surfer, but a big-wave rider too, so I have a lot of respect for him. Just before the heat I came up to him and I had all this green stuff, that Barley Green powder stuff, in and around my mouth. It's good energy food and I usually have a mouthful of it before heats, but it can look a bit messy or weird to people who don't know what it is. Joel just looked at me, screwed up his nose and said, 'What's that?' I only half heard him, because at the same time I said, 'Let's toss for priority.' 'Priority' is who has the right to the first wave of the heat. Normally it's decided by hassling, positioning and allocation by the head judge, but with close friends some of us have the tradition of gentleman's rules, tossing for initial priority and taking turns thereafter, instead of hassling.

Joel and I are kind of close as surfing 'brothers', so I thought it was a good thing to offer, but in retrospect I shouldn't have done it. I didn't really think hard enough about it. Darren Handley and a few crew were all standing around, and Taj Burrow was there with Joel, who already had his competition vest on, ready to go. He just looked at me and said, 'I don't think so.' Straightaway I thought, 'Strewth, I shouldn't have said that.' As the confident kid he is, and I *was*, I should have known better. So, at the start of the heat, I did hassle him.

Joel virtually grew up under the rock at Snapper. Jumping off the outside rock up there in a swell is a real delicate moment. Joel jumps like a professional bungee jumper, cockily confident every time, and his surfing … well, it's just ridiculous what he does out there. I knew that I had my work cut out for me like never before.

I think I got the inside position to start with. We were sitting in over near the jump-off rock. A wave came wide and jacked, and Joel reared up and paddled for it. He's got long arms, like Margo, and somehow he crossed the 20 metres from where we were sitting and into that wave in a matter of seconds. He got an 8.5. I was thinking, 'Oh, oh, here we go!' I got the next wave and it didn't even do half of what his did, and my board felt hopeless. I was way too flustered, and when I'm like that I try way too hard.

I reckon that's why I do well in skins events. The more tired I get, the better I perform. I'm *feeling* the wave, the board, the power, and that's when I surf my best. When I'm pumped I'm no good. That's why I don't listen to all that heavy metal music. I'm always listening to Coast FM and really nice soft songs, so I can stay calm and blend in with the waves. That mightn't make sense to a lot of people. Most think you've got to be amped to do good, but in my case, it's the opposite.

Anyway, for the rest of that heat I felt I was surfing pretty well. I watched it on video later and thought I was doing OK, though the board wasn't really looking good at all. I was trying to surf critically because the judging format had changed the week before the contest, and that was what they were now awarding points for. I don't think they really knew what they were doing that day, though, or even the whole event. I was trying to go for big moves, which you do anyway when the waves are good. You just surf it, and don't worry about grovelling.

So Joel's waves generally seemed to go longer than mine, and he was grovelling good on the ones that were going right through, and getting the scores. I felt like I was surfing a lot better than how it looked like on video, but I think it was just that the board wouldn't give it to me. Sometimes you feel like you are surfing really good, but then you see the video and you realise you weren't surfing well at all. Other times you feel like you're not surfing well at all, and you come in to the beach and someone is all stoked, saying, 'Your board was going unreal.' Then when you see yourself on TV you're going, 'Yeah!' Nothing is constant.

Anyway, they were throwing big scores at Joel and, I guess, expecting me to match him, but my waves weren't like Joel's. The waves I got didn't give me a chance to win the heat. Maybe a couple of my waves were underscored, but I was basically comboed (i.e. needing two waves to catch up) after Joel's first three rides for the remainder of the heat.

As I got out of the water, I was feeling pretty upset, and even though I'd lost, some big guy came up and gave me a hug. Maybe he gave me a hug for winning the world title last year; I don't know. I swear, to this day I've had more congratulations than anyone ever. I've really been honoured by everyone's support. There's just been so much out there, and I love it.

I got surrounded by the press and TV cameras after they'd finished mobbing Joel, and it was pretty hard to keep a stiff upper lip. After all the training I'd done and that, it was a hard pill to swallow, but I had to face the media throng. As far as the Billabong Pro was concerned, nothing had changed for me. I've been knocked out of the event early for the last, how many I don't know, years since the event began. It's always been like that. As I walked up the beach I just wanted to get out of there, but I ended up hanging for a bit, getting my money and watching a few heats. Bea had gone to Bali earlier in the week, so I had no one to go home to. I just waited until a respectable time to open a can of beer, maybe about 3 pm, and then started drinking and forgot about how I was feeling. I had a fairly big night.

THURSDAY 16 > SATURDAY 18

FOR THE REST OF the Billabong event I basically turned into a bit of a nocturnal social host. As we travel around the world, surfers from the areas we are visiting sometimes take us out to their local nightspots. It's usually on the last night of the event, or on the night you lose your heat — whichever comes first. Often, your first instinct upon losing is to let your hair down. Needless to say, the Gold Coast has plenty of entertaining nightspots, and since I was knocked out of the event, I saw it as my duty, as a local, to show a few of the boys around town. Besides that, the Aussie guys have always been keen to have a good time. I'm on top of the rankings right now, so I have more than enough reason to celebrate, but my little party crew of Hoyo (Matt Hoy), Dooma

(Damien Hardman), Beau Emerton, Powelly (Mike Powell) and Luke Egan sure know how to have a good time, whatever the situation. People sometimes think we overdo it, but we're just having a good time.

We hit the town in Surfers Paradise, of course, and went to Jupiter's Casino. I love casinos. One night I took Kalani Robb, Taylor Knox, John Shimooka, and a few crew out to Jupiter's. I was stoked to have them on my turf. Perhaps I had a few beers too many, but I was trying to show Kalani how good I was at blackjack and betting $200 to $300 a hand, and not winning a thing. Then I tried doubling up to win it back but, as always happens in these sorts of situations, I just kept losing. I lost about $2000 in ten minutes, and Kalani was just laughing, going, 'Geez, Occ. You're really good at this!'

I love hanging with Kalani. He's been on the circuit for quite a few years now, but he's still a grommet at heart. He's so much fun; a really good kid. Well he's not a kid anymore, but he's so full of energy you'd be easily mistaken. Taylor is cool too. He's about the nicest American I know. He's a straight-up guy, just like an Aussie, and his surfing is far out. He just rips. He puts his board so on the rail, and has such a good rhythm with the wave. I just love his surfing. I don't know how he fell out of the top 44 a couple of years back, but it's just unreal that he's back in there this year.

I didn't return to the contest, not even to the presentation night. It was the last place I wanted to be. When you lose, you just don't want to know about the competition scene. Luke Egan made the quarters, and I wanted to be there for him, but the social schedule had taken a toll on me. I saw Luke the night before the final day of the Billabong Pro, and I told him that the only way I was going out again the next night was if he won the contest. I was trying to psych him up, but he reckoned he was going to make me go out, whatever the result. I really wanted Luke to win, but he didn't. I saw the TV footage later, and the waves looked pretty average; it dropped a lot during the day. It was a great win for Sunny Garcia, though. He was quoted on the news saying, 'I want Occy's title.' He made a call and that's great. I had already said before the season that he was going to be a contender, and he knows he's up for it. He's been training really hard and everything has been going his way. I am stoked for him. I like the fact that he mentioned my name, too. I thought that was really nice.

SUNDAY 19

RECOVERY DAY. Like many days spent at home, I just kicked back and watched the weekend's league games. I love footy, and I decided a while back to spoil myself with one of those big flatscreen televisions. I love watching it in my big armchair, just cruising in my own space in our beautiful home. I did fit a surf in between telecasts, taking Russell Winter down to Fingal. The waves were beautiful, only about three foot, but they were good. Luke rang me later and said he was leaving the next day for the Mark Richards Newcastle City Pro WQS, and I was like, 'I'm with ya! Let's go.'

MONDAY 20

WOKE UP EARLY, PACKED MY bag and boards, and jumped in the car with Luke. He really likes his cars, and has several. This one was a cool Ford Falcon panel van. It was a rainy day. A cold front had moved north through Sydney and Newcastle and we were driving right into the teeth of it — not helped by the fact that the motor on Luke's windscreen wipers was broken, and it was making the most godawful noise. All day long on the highway, we had to listen to it screech and scrape. We had to push the volume up on the stereo to like 30, just to drown out the noise. Luke didn't like that at all. We drove for about five hours or so down to Coffs Harbour and had a surf there in the pouring rain. These six little grommets sat watching us, drenched and dripping wet, just so happy that we were surfing their local beach. They couldn't believe it. It took me back to when I was a grommet, in the days before I started competing in big contests. I remember all the pros coming to Cronulla for the Straight Talk Tyres event, and sitting there with my mates watching Mark Richards surf 'our' waves. It was awesome.

I actually had a really good surf at Coffs, on a new board. I had just taken a few backup boards down for Newcastle, thinking I'd save my good boards, but then I realised that the ones I had were my good boards. I'd taken along a new Dahlberg six-channel to try out, and there, my first time on it, it just went mad. I was like, 'You're kidding me! Why haven't I been riding this thing all along?' I was stoked. Afterwards, we drove for another couple of hours with the windscreen wipers going full blast and driving us mad, before stopping at Kempsey. We stayed the night at a rickety old hotel, with KFC and a big bottle of Coke for dinner. It was good, just what I needed. I love fried chicken. As a grommet, and later on when I should have known better, I used to eat heaps of it. There was a shop that sold it right next to my home where I grew up at Kurnell. I think I was probably their best customer.

TUESDAY 21

WE WOKE UP AND got back on the road the next morning. It was still raining, pouring in fact, and we had to listen to the bung windscreen wipers again. We drove quite a distance to one of Luke's secret spots. He was all excited because the wind had been blowing all night from the right direction, with the rain. Luke rang Matt Hoy on the way there, and got him out of bed to run down to Merewether and check the wind and swell directions. Matt rang back, saying it all looked good. Both of them were amping, and the thought that I was going to surf a good left that doesn't work well too often got me keen too. Joel Parkinson was ahead of us down the highway in his new black beast of a Commodore, so we rang him and told him to slow down, and where to pull off. How good are mobile phones for coordinating surf trips!? We met him at a site above the secret spot from where you can check the waves but, as it was rainy, visibility was limited. We ended up checking it down on the beach, and even though it looked like maybe there wasn't enough swell, we decided to hike the couple of kilometres in anyway. We donned our wetsuits, Luke grabbed a backpack, and away we went.

I ran the whole way. Luke and Joel ran half the distance with me, but then started walking. Once I start running, I can't stop.

When I got there, the wind was howling offshore. Luke's spot was happening. The waves looked really fun. It was like 2–3', a perfectly peeling left-hander. Amazing, because every other beach on the way down that day had been like 8–10' and onshore. It was really special. I was actually pretty scared, because when the tide went out the rip started running superfast and strong. It was radical. If you went outside the take-off area, you would be sucked out and you wouldn't be able to get back in. It actually happened to some other guys that same afternoon. They were picked up about three kilometres out to sea by a rescue helicopter.

As the tide ran out, the waves went from being 2–3' to 6–8'. I was taking sets on the head because I didn't want to get caught in the rip. It was like an express train — a really strong rip way too strong to paddle against. I was ducking in because the sets weren't that good. The medium-sized ones were better. One set literally broke right on my head and I was gripping my board, freaking, as it hit me. It took me right to the bottom and just held me there. It eventually got too big and dangerous so we came in. There were only two other guys out, five of us on a perfect left-hand break. They were telling us not to reveal the spot to anyone, and we assured them we wouldn't. They had a 4WD, and we started talking to them, thinking we were going to score a lift out of there, but they didn't even offer one, so we trudged back in the rain. It was sure worth it, though.

After a bit of a smoke-'em-up session with a few doughnuts (Luke can't help himself) in the muddy carpark, Luke and I got back on the highway and headed on down to Newcastle. When we got there late that afternoon we checked into the hotel on the beach and surfed at Nobby's. It was about 6–8', and we both had a couple of good big barrels. It was a great day of surfing for me. Luke was going mad, surfing so good. Peter McCabe was out there too. He's an old shaping and charging legend from Newcastle, one of the pioneers of the early days in Bali. Nobby's is his local spot. It was good to see him. Later, Luke and I had a really nice dinner, and then went out for a couple of beers. What a day!

WEDNESDAY 22

IT WAS STILL RAINING when I woke up, hardly having stopped at all overnight. I had two quick little onshore surfs, but basically I just stayed in my hotel room most of the day, sleeping and watching movies. Luke rang me at some stage to say he didn't feel like doing anything or driving anywhere.

I had to do some Oakley promos late in the day. All the in-store promos we do lately seem to be so crowded. The one that night was at a shopping mall, and it was pretty hectic. It seemed like there were thousands of kids wanting to get their posters signed. They kept pressing and pushing against the table we were all sitting at, signing this and that. In the end we were almost pinned to the wall behind us.

THURSDAY 23

A BEAUTIFUL MORNING. The rain was gone and the waves were really good — offshore too.

One of this year's features and highlights of the Newcastle event was the Champion of Champions dinner. Kelly and all the world champs since 1976 were coming for it, including my mate Derek Ho. I didn't think he'd turn up, because at this time of year it's good late season in Hawaii, when Pipe can regularly be 10–15' and clean. When they said he was coming I thought, 'Yeah, I'll believe that when I see it.' As it turned out, he did indeed come, and ended up staying in the room next to mine. I didn't even know. He knocked on my door, and I asked, 'Who is it?' There was no response, so I asked again. He replied, 'Johnny.' I thought it was John Shimooka, but when I opened the door it was Derek. We gave each other a big hug and talked for an hour or so, and then I suggested we go surfing because the waves were so good.

We went down to Dixon Park, a couple of kilometres down towards Merewether. I couldn't believe it. We pulled up and it was just perfect, like tubing Narrabeen. We were out there immediately and had a great surf for a couple of hours. Derek had an unbelievable stand-up barrel, so long and so nice. I had a really good surf myself. It was great! We came back to the hotel, hung out for a while, and then I took him surfing at Nobby's. He wore a steamer and was boiling, but I do that all the time, wearing a steamer almost every day. The third surf of the day was at Newcastle Beach that night, to get familiar with the contest wave. It was another good day, although the weather turned foul again late in the day. I just quietly cruised that night.

FRIDAY 24

ANOTHER WET AND MISERABLE morning, too wet to go anywhere or do anything. I relaxed most of the day, knowing we had another promo that afternoon up the coast, a good hour or more's drive. I assumed Luke and I would drive up there, but he rang up after lunch and announced he didn't feel like driving, and that we were going to fly up by helicopter. The Newcastle Knights, the local first grade rugby league team, were playing that night, and we wanted to get back from the promo to go to the football in time for the kick-off. It wouldn't have been possible in a car, so the chopper was good for that. I'd never been in a helicopter before so I was kind of hesitant, but Luke took me aside and said that when he took me snowboarding later in they year I'd need to know what a chopper was like. I swear it was blowing like 50 knots, quite bumpy, and I didn't like it that much.

Anyway, we did the promo, fully packed out again, and then flew back down to Marathon Stadium. I'd lost my ticket to get in so I asked the pilot, one of Luke's mates, if he could land us on the centre field, but he couldn't, obviously. He landed us in a paddock just near it, right across the road from McDonalds. I'm sure everyone looking on thought there was an emergency or something, but then out jumps Occy and Louie. It turned out one of the guys who ran the security at the surf contest was the local Chief of Police or something, so the next thing we knew a police car rocked up to collect us as we walked into the Maccas carpark on our way to get a feed. It was classic. Some grommets recognised us as we were getting into the police car. They probably thought we were being arrested. Anyway, the cops dutifully whisked us off to the football.

All the world champs were supposed to be at the game, but only Martin Potter and I ended up fronting. Newcastle were playing St George Illawarra, who are the neighbouring team to the Cronulla Sutherland team, the Sharks. Todd Prestage was in the VIP box that they'd arranged for us. He's a fanatical St George supporter, and he asked me who I was backing in the game, assuming probably that it'd be the Dragons. I don't think he was too impressed when I said Newcastle. The Sharks and St George are longtime rivals. Being from Cronulla, it was only natural for me to not back the Dragons.

After the game we went out for a drink with Andrew Johns, who's a deadset legend, and a few of his teammates. Luke was there too, of course, but he let slip that every time he'd been to a Newcastle Knights home game and watched from a VIP box, the local team had lost. All the Knights players turned around and said, 'You're never coming to a home game again. If you do, you've got to sit outside on the grass hill.' Louie laughed, but I think he was a bit crushed.

SATURDAY 25

I HAD TO SURF IN the contest the next morning, which was unfortunate because I was still a bit hungover from the beers with the footy crew. I still had the wobbly boot on. On my first few waves I was falling flat on my face, but right at the end I caught a right-hander and did what I thought were two really good turns. It was a short wave but it must have scored some points. With 30 seconds to go, and apparently needing a decent score, I got a good wave and did two really big turns and got swept through the heat. All the Brazilians were spewing because they thought I hadn't surfed well enough to get through. But I did the moves, and the judging criterion has changed this year to favour bigger moves rather than soft manoeuvres for length of ride. I was so not into the Brazilian calls because they don't go for big moves. I don't mind the way they surf, but they don't go big; they just stay on their boards and play the formula. They obviously can't understand the new judging criterion, but they will soon. Most of us really appreciate the judging changes. I didn't care what the Brazilians thought anyway. I was just stoked that I got through with some big moves.

I went back to my room and rested most of the afternoon and then had a really good heat with Matt Hoy, Shane Wehner and another guy whose name escapes me. I won and I was stoked. I then had to go to Mark Richards's house at Merewether and sign something like 650 posters for the Champion of Champions dinner, to raise money for a Sudden Infant Death Syndrome charity. My wrist wore out, and I don't think I finished signing them all, but MR said he'd send me the rest to finish the job. After that, we had group photos taken with all the other champs, and then had to go get ready and go to the dinner.

There were about 500 people at the function and there was a great spirit in the room. The night started with a video compilation in which all the world champions had a little section each. Of course, as reigning world champion, I came up last on the screen. It felt really weird — 'Oh yeah, I'm a world champion!' It may seem a strange thing to say, but winning the world title obviously doesn't change who or what you are. At functions like that though, the fact that you are a world champ really sort of sinks in. You can't really explain it.

After the video presentation we were asked to come up on the stage in groups of four, as though we were sitting around in someone's loungeroom having a chat, and answer questions. It was great. Everyone was really relaxed. The first group — MR, Rabbit Bartholomew, Shaun Tomson and Peter Townend — was so entertaining. I really enjoyed the stories they told. When it was my turn to get up, I wasn't sure whether I would have rather watched myself up there than be up there.

Everyone had a big night, but for something completely different, I was responsible and got to bed by about midnight. I took it really easy on the beers and stuff. Hoyo and all the boys kicked on. Even Luke stayed longer than me, which is unusual. He's usually more responsible than me; than most of us actually. Deep down I had the urge to party but I really wanted to win the event.

SUNDAY 26

I WOKE UP FEELING good, had an early surf and got some good turns in. I then went for my heat, but unfortunately I didn't get through. I was trying too hard, which is not a normal thing for me, but on the rare occasions that I do try too hard I mess up. Anyway, it was alright; it wasn't the end of the world. I knew we had a big expression session coming up that afternoon with all the world champs, so I went back to my room, watched some heats from up there, had some lunch and snoozed off.

Next thing, MR, I think, was knocking at my door, saying, 'Could you just come down and sign some things?' I think I might have nodded off, because next thing the previous night's compere, former *Tracks* editor Neil Ridgway, was on the phone asking me to come downstairs. I dawdled down, walked around a corner and straight into a full-blown press conference. I couldn't believe it. It seemed as if there were hundreds of people in attendance. All the guys had to sign hundreds of posters. The press conference went for over an hour, TV cameras and microphones and all, and it was a bit anxious in the end; quite a different matter from cruising downstairs assuming I was going to sign a 'few things'. However, I didn't mind. We had a group photo done too. silverchair's Ben Gillies had paid $5000 in a charity auction the night before to have his photo taken with all the world champs, so it was a real pleasure posing with him for that one. I love Ben, and his band, and it was good to talk to him for a while after the photographer had wrapped up.

The expression session that afternoon was special, a really nice feeling, and the crowd on the beach was massive; more like a football crowd. All week there'd been no more than 2000 people on the beach, but that afternoon there must have been at least 20 000 people there.

After we'd all jumped off the rocks and paddled into the line-up, Barton Lynch and I turned and looked onto the beach and were both stunned by the size of the crowd. For a second my mind flashed back to 1986 when I beat Tom Curren here in the BHP International. The crowd that day was massive too. It was outrageous. The memory gave me a big shot of adrenalin and then a wave came. I felt my first turn was a really good one, but it all went a bit downhill in performance level after that, though I got out of the water still feeling quite charged. I imagine it feels something like how a musician in a big band might feel walking offstage after just having finished a concert or something.

After such a good weekend, it goes without saying that we had to have a beer to celebrate. Hoyo wanted me to drag all the world champs to his favourite pub, the Burwood Inn at the back of Merewether, but not many of them were into it. It's the best pub in Newy, just ask Hoyo; except he'll tell you that it's the best pub in the *world.* It is a really good pub, and the publican Bazza is a great host. They call it 'The Zoo'. Tom Carroll, Kelly Slater and I rocked up and found Hoyo and Andrew Johns in a state you'd expect after spending most of the afternoon on the Tooheys. We got on the piss with them, sunk a few schooners, and generally had a laugh. It was good, a great wind-down after an entertaining and eventful weekend. I eventually grabbed a pizza on the way back to my motel and just crashed out, exhausted.

MONDAY 27 › WEDNESDAY 29

SOMEHOW I'D ORGANISED for Mark Richards to collect me and take me to the airport the next morning. How's that? MR as your chauffeur! Reliable as ever, he turned up on my doorstep at 6.30 am on the dot, helped me pack my boards, and drove me to the Williamtown base where my Impulse flight was waiting for me. Needless to say, I had to sign more posters on the way. Luke was on the same flight. When I got home, I did nothing for the rest of the day; just relaxed after the big weekend.

On the Tuesday I went down to the back beach at Fingal and did a couple of beach runs, which eventually made me feel revitalised. I got a few games of golf in over this period too, which was good. I also took delivery of a few new Dahlberg channel bottoms.

THURSDAY 30

LUKE AND I FLEW to Perth to compete in the Wet Dreams Margaret River Masters. We had two promos to do in the city, so we went straight from the airport and booked into the casino there. We had a really nice lunch; we just cruised, talking about the big waves that we hoped we'd get down at Margarets. The forecast was for big swell. We had our fingers crossed. We had a Billabong in-store promo to do at 3 pm, for which Taj Burrow drove up all the way from Margaret River. It was unbelievable that he had to drive three hours to do a promo! It was huge, though; there must have been thousands of grommets there. It was so crowded we only got through signing posters for about half the kids. I then had an Oakley promo to do after that, which wasn't as crowded, but was still pretty hectic. Oakley's John Shimooka then took us to dinner at a really nice Japanese restaurant at the casino. I love Japanese food.

Later, when we were out on the casino floor, Luke came up and joked that he was going to show me how to play blackjack. Instead, I taught him how to lose $200 in two minutes, and I lost $500 in five minutes. I wanted to see if we could win quick, but sometimes when you try to win quick, you lose quicker. Luke wasn't impressed: 'I don't like this game!' I assured him it would grow on him, but he didn't seem too convinced.

FRIDAY 31

JOHN SHIMOOKA STAYED OVERNIGHT at the casino, so when we all woke up we jumped in our rental cars and followed each other down the coast. Louie and Shmoo were hanging for a coffee so we stopped for an espresso. I actually had a coffee … I couldn't believe it! I never drink coffee. It was a beautiful day, but a really cold morning, so I figured the coffee would warm me up. I had to have sugar in it though, but there wasn't any. I ended up having to buy a two-kilo bag of brown sugar, just to have a teaspoon of it. Luke and Shmoo just couldn't stop laughing at me. Anyway I drank the coffee, and it made me feel weird. I had to keep going to the toilet all the way down there. That stopped them laughing.

The car was packed with boards, so we couldn't really see each other. I was supposed to be acting as co-pilot, but I was on the nod, and kept snoozing. We'd heard the previous day that the waves were about six foot, which we were amped for, but then on the way down we heard that the swell had dropped off. We checked into the motel we usually stay at, The Captain Freycinet, unpacked, and then went for a nice surf near Ellensbrook, which is north of Margaret River. We progressively paddled along, surfing three different reefs. Luke was surfing good, but I was riding a new board shaped by someone other than Rodney Dahlberg, and it wasn't really working for me. I was tired too, so I got out and sat on the beach and watched. There were a couple of American surfers out there with Luke, twin brothers C. J. and Damien Hobgood. I don't know which one is which, but they were ripping. It was marginal surf, breaking close to the rocks, but they didn't care. They were making almost everything they tried — aerials, aerial 360s, you name it. I was really impressed. I think their energy might have even worn me out actually, because we went back to the motel after that and had a nap.

I love coming to Margaret River! I've been going there since I was a little grommet, surfing in the schoolboys Under-15 division. It's an excellent place to go and recoup and eat well, rest and *surf, surf, surf.* We kept resting that afternoon, and went for a surf late in the afternoon at the contest site. The waves were pretty fun. I tried a new channel bottom for the first time, and it went really, really good. We went back and had dinner and then I went to sleep. A pretty mellow day.

april 2000

April

>>>> SATURDAY 1

WE WERE UP BEFORE dawn, so we went down to the contest site at Surfers Point to get a warm-up surf before the first heats later in the day. The line-up was just *packed.* I won my heat riding that new board. I was treating it like a baby because it was going so good. I was even trying to pull back on some of my turns so I wouldn't hurt it. I didn't want to surf it too heavily.

Unfortunately, Luke got knocked out in his first heat, so he was a bit upset. He surfed well, but was short a wave. We went back to the hotel and hung out. Luke is involved in the development of a new sunglasses company called Electric, and that night he was taking a few of the Team Electric grommets out for dinner. I know I'm sponsored by Oakley, but I played grommet for a night, spy maybe, and tagged along for the feed. It was fun. We had a really nice dinner. Luke then went out to watch some bands after that at the local rock festival at the football field, and I went home to the motel to catch some shuteye.

SUNDAY 2

I WOKE UP EARLY, as always, feeling good and totally on track for a good result. It was a great day, even though the waves were only 2–3', which is really, really small for Margaret River. I got through my heat surfing a 6'5" board, but then, unfortunately, I cracked a fin. I discovered it just before my quarter-final; I didn't have time to get another board. Luke threw on a wettie and went caddy for me with one of his boards at the ready, but somehow I managed with the fin half hanging out. I actually won the heat — one of my waves was an 8.0.

Luke told me my board had looked alright, but that it had felt a bit weird. Just before my semi-final I had a look at it, and not only had I cracked one fin, I had cracked all three. Even the back fin was out. It was impossible to ride. With just 15 minutes till my heat hit the water, I was totally stressing. Luke jumped in the car and tore back to town. It's about a 15-minute drive into Margarets township, and it was a Sunday, with heaps of traffic around. But somehow he got there and back in time, with a replacement board. It was a different board that I wasn't too sure about, from a different shaper, but I had no choice. As it turned out, I couldn't even surf the thing. I couldn't even find the right spot to stand on it. Suffice it to say, I lost. Taj Burrow went absolutely mad in the final, just blitzing, but then got an interference, and Mark Bannister eventually won. Good luck to him. We watched the final from the carpark and then bolted back to the motel to do a flying pack job. We were driving out of town within 20 minutes and heading back towards Perth and the casino.

We were booked on a midnight flight out of Perth, and so rather than just hang out in the Qantas Club, we returned our rental car, checked in our bags, got our boarding passes and then went straight to the casino. Very conveniently, it's only about a five-minute drive from the airport. There was quite a crew of us there, including Richie Lovett, Todd Prestage and a few others. We all won money. Of course, the only trouble is if you're sitting on a good hand, it's impossible to leave. However, since we'd already checked in our bags, the plane was never going to leave without us. We all jetted out of there smiling because Margaret River always provides, one way or another, a good, reviving and restful week. It's a great place.

MONDAY 3

I GOT BACK TO the Gold Coast mid-morning, after the overnight 'red-eye' flight. It's a bit tough sometimes, all this travelling business. I had just one day to try and kick back at home, see Bea, do this and that, organise boards, and then get back on a plane to Sydney to go to the Konica Skins at Sandon Point, in the northern suburbs of Wollongong. It's just a jam-packed schedule sometimes. No matter how tight it is though, it's always great to get home and recharge. I just love being home.

TUESDAY 4

I FLEW DOWN TO Sydney around lunchtime, hired a car and headed south for Wollongong. I had to go via my old Cronulla stomping ground, because that's the only way I know how to get down there. We had a promo draw for the event at a shopping mall in Wollongong, and I made it there just in time. It was a bit of a hoax. Every year they say, 'You've got to be there for the draw, you've got to be there,' but every year we wander away at the end of it, thinking, 'Why did we have to be there?' It's just a media thing, I guess.

After the draw we went back and checked in at the Novotel at North Beach, where we always stay when in the 'Gong for the Skins. Luke, Hoyo and I all ended up in adjoining rooms. That kind of gave us the sense that we were all in for a big week. We had a quiet night though, relaxing over a nice dinner, and then crashed early.

WEDNESDAY 5

THE NEXT MORNING WE were bummed to see the surf was only about one foot. Instantly we all thought, 'Bummer, we could still be at home and not be missing a thing.' We'd already heard that the trials for the event had yet to be run, so we were going to be sitting around for that as well. We ended up going for a surf at Woonona, and there we ran into a local identity named Barry Stace. He's been looking after the grommets down there since I was a grommet, so it was really good to see him. He's a really mellow and unassuming guy, with a good heart. Speaking of grommets, Hoyo was ripping out there like … a grommet.

The night before, in the lobby of the Novotel, I had run into a guy called Graham McNeice. He used to host sports shows for Channel Ten, and once worked closely with a guy called Brian Walsh, producer of the old 2SM Coca-Cola Surfabout events. Graham now works for Sky TV, who are a big sports cable-TV outfit. We got talking and he mentioned that there was a big raceday on at Kembla Grange, which is a couple of clicks down the road from Wollongong. Hoyo, who likes the races and trots, chipped in and said, 'We're there!' and Graham, who obviously has plenty of contacts in the racing industry, gave us a number to call if we wanted to go.

Sitting out the back in the surf at Woonona, Hoyo looked over and announced, 'We're going to the races!' and I was like, 'Let's go!' It was about midday by the time we left Woonona and we drove into downtown Wollongong and walked straight into some shop called Mensland. We both slapped a couple of hundred dollars on the counter, and within about five minutes both walked out carrying a suit. The sales guy couldn't believe it. We were going to the races, all dressed up so that we could hobnob it in the Members' Enclosure. What a great day it turned out to be … well, great day *and* night. It was a big one. After the track we went out to dinner. We all knew the surf hadn't got any bigger by dark, so the odds were we weren't going to have the contest the next day anyway.

THURSDAY 6

I WOKE UP RATHER slovenly the next morning at about 8.30 or 9 am, routinely pulled back the curtains and was absolutely horrified to look out over a stormy sea with eight-foot waves crashing onto North Beach. I was instantly filled with panic and semi-screamed to myself, 'Oh no! No! The contest will be on!' I knew I was in an early heat so I was stressing big-time. I ran out the door to Hoyo's room and banged on the door, but there was

no response. I got Luke up, rang Hoyo's room and woke him up, and then together we all raced up to Sandon Point.

When we got there we were confused because the carpark wasn't packed, like it is when the contest is on. Luckily, the contest wasn't on. We would have missed our heats but the same stormfront that had brought up the swell unexpectedly, had also ripped the contest tents and the whole set-up to shreds. It looked like a bomb had gone off in the official area. We were so relieved that we were jumping around hugging each other and giving high-fives. We were just so lucky. After that drama we just slinked back to the hotel, relaxed and had a very quiet day.

FRIDAY 7

WE WERE STILL RECUPERATING the next morning, but had to shape up quickly to get ready for the early start. We were certainly a whole lot better prepared than the previous day. The surf was a decent 3–5' and quite contestable, though there were some strange lulls. The contest format works via three-man heats. You get to pick three waves and after the completion of each wave, first, second or third, you raise your arms to nominate that wave as your claim. Once you nominate your wave you have to get out and leave the line-up to the other two guys you're surfing against, hoping that they don't better what you've scored. If you win, you get $4000, and you're back out there for the next heat against two new guys. It's an exciting format, and good fun. You can surf just one wave, in the first few minutes if you're lucky, and then get out. Hoyo won his first heat and $4000, and then I was in the next heat with him. I won it (sorry Matt), and also the heat after that, but then I got knocked out. It didn't worry me too much. I'd won $8000 for just two heats.

In the second round I really got a roll going, mostly getting a wave in the first minute and then getting out. For a while there they just couldn't get me out. I ended up winning $28 000. Needless to say, I was stoked. Thank you, Konica! Luke, Hoyo, Law, Sarge and myself went into town that night for dinner to celebrate; obviously, it was my shout. We wanted to have Japanese; we all do on tour. We went to one restaurant but it looked too 'Aussie', so we jumped in some taxis and went to another one right in the centre of town. It was only average though. It was BYO too, so Hoyo did the bolt down to the corner pub and brought back a carton of Carlton Cold and some wine. We only drank about half the carton. Our next stop was a pub that local ironmen Darren and Dean Mercer have a stake in, so we decided we'd give the rest of the carton away as we walked to the Mercers' place. You wouldn't believe how hard it was to give away a dozen beers and a bottle of wine! We eventually found a couple of women in their thirties who took them, but not before they asked, 'Are they cold?' People are so weird sometimes.

The Mercers' pub was great, packed out too. Deano was the ultimate host. He just kept bringing trays of bourbon and cokes. He'll never make a profit as a publican if that's how he operates. Lots of the crew from the contest were there that night, including Michael Lowe who was very happy with having won about $16 000 himself. It was good to see a local lad do good in his own area. He's a good man, Michael, and a gutsy surfer too.

SATURDAY 8

WE HAD TO BACK up the next day back at Sandon for a doubles contest, one guy and one chick. The surf had dropped to half the size of the previous day, and was almost dangerous, breaking really close to the rocks. Frankly, there were plenty among us that just didn't want to be there. If they do it again next year they should put the doubles on the first day as a build-up to the main event. I was teamed with women's world champ Layne Beachley, and before we'd even paddled out, I told her, 'You're not going to get any money with me today.' She wasn't happy. I had to go through the motions, though, and surfed two heats before getting knocked out. I just wanted to go home, and so did the locals. There was hardly anybody watching. It was such an anti-climax.

Back at the hotel, Hoyo pointed out it was raceday, so we went to the pub and bet on the horses. The boys were spewing at me because after winning $28 000 I couldn't lose on the horses either. Worse, I was a complete novice at betting. They even had to show me how to fill out the TAB slips, but almost every horse I picked won. Hoyo was like, 'You can't do this!' It was such a funny afternoon. I bet on one horse called Sky Beau just because Beau Emerton has the same name. After placing the bet, I rang him on his mobile to tell him I was backing 'him'. Beau was driving back to Forster from the contest and, knowing the horse, chuckled, 'Don't worry about it, it's never won a race!' The moment he said that, Sky Beau crossed the line first and paid like $33 and I'd bet $20 on it. We kept getting interrupted at the pub that afternoon by local crew wanting us to sign schooner glasses and stuff. It was such a funny afternoon.

SUNDAY 9

MOST OF THE BOYS went home in the morning, so I spent much of the day just slothing, watching movies and sleeping. Mid afternoon, I met with Sarge for a few beers over the tape recorder to bring this diary up to date, and then went back to just hanging out, waiting for the presentation function. It was a quiet affair. I went and collected my money from the contest, as well as Hoy's and Beau's, and then went back to the hotel to pack and go to sleep early.

MONDAY 10 › SATURDAY 15

THE FOLLOWING MORNING, I only just made my flight back to the Gold Coast after getting caught in the Sydney peak-hour traffic. I just can't believe Sydney now, it's so crowded and chaotic. I sure I couldn't live there anymore. It was great knowing I was flying back to the Goldy, and our beautiful home and space up at Bilambil.

Back on the Gold Coast, after having won the Konica Skins at Sandon Point, it was time for more backslaps and shaking of hands. I was congratulated all over again, everywhere I went. Don't get me wrong, I totally love the support I get from everybody, all around Australia. I was still getting congratulations aplenty from winning the world title, though, and that was almost six months previous. Now I was getting congratulated again, this time for the Skins. Truly, I was stoked, but it seemed really funny too. I was thinking 'Here we go again!' Even though the Konica Skins had only been what we call a 'specialty' event, that is, there's no Championship points attached to it, it was the first thing I'd won since the world title. It was really good for my self-esteem and confidence.

One of my immediate priorities when I got home was to get Rodney Dahlberg to shape me some more channel-bottomed surfboards. I loved the one I'd ridden to the semi-finals at Margaret River, then I'd won the Konica on one, and the third one remained in cotton wool (not literally) at home.

In the week I was home before Bells I didn't do too much, other than relax. I rode the two channel bottoms I'd already broken in a bit down at Fingal. Unfortunately, there wasn't much swell that week, so I was training more than surfing. It was great to just be there though, basically all alone too, because it was bloody cold. The water was freezing, and the air was cold too. Just the way I like it! Usually it means swell is coming when it's cold but, as I said, we didn't get any.

I had a swing on the golf clubs on the Wednesday of that week too, but I needn't have bothered. I had a shocker. It was a club comp, but I guess my mind was occupied with other things. I couldn't get more than 20 points. It was a bit frustrating, but my golf mates loved it because they got all my money.

I also went to a new bar and restaurant opening down at Coolangatta that week. A friend of mine opened it. It's called the Stella Maris, after the famous guesthouse that used to be on the beachfront there. The Pointes North apartment block stands there now, and the bar is on street level under it. It's a great bar, with good food, and there's all sorts of local surfing memorabilia around the walls. I gave my friend the signed and framed picture of the 12 world champs from Newcastle to hang up that night. He was stoked. I've got to lend him a few other boards and things as well.

It was good to eat out that night too. We continually eat out at restaurants when we're on the road, but at home it's rare for me to go out at night, especially to eat, because I married one of the best cooks on earth. My wife Bea is such a good cook. Guess what? I've even been cooking a bit lately. I cooked a roast last night. Hard work that!

Bea has been busy establishing a new business for herself. It's fair enough, because her life has just been so totally dominated by mine in recent years. She's always been right there behind me in my world title quest. Now she's trying to start a business with a friend, importing furniture and artifacts from all around the world and places like Marrakech and Italy. She's got incredibly good taste and skills as an interior decorator, so I reckon she's cut out for that business.

SUNDAY 16

WITH A BIG BAG FULL of nice new winter clothes that I'd collected from Billabong the previous week, and an awesome new steamer, I headed for Coolangatta airport, and the annual Rip Curl Pro at Bells Beach in Victoria. The word before we left was that they were expecting big swell down there, so I packed some big boards in anticipation. I took two bulging board bags, six boards in each, so I was equipped for anything. I love Bells.

My regular travelling buddy, Luke Egan, was on a flight before mine, so when I landed in Melbourne, collected my rental car, and started heading south towards Torquay, I phoned him on his mobile to see what the surf was like. That was pretty silly though, because it's more than an hour's drive from Melbourne to Torquay. In fact, he was only 30 minutes down the road ahead of me. As we had a laugh on our mobiles, I tried to catch him, but Louie isn't the slowest of drivers, so there was no hope. Towards the end of our phone conversation he was pulling into the driveway where he always stays in Bells. His host is the Victorian state sales rep for Billabong, Andrew Flinton, and a good friend of mine too.

I always stay in a house right near the shops at Torquay owned by former Oakley Australia owner, Steve Perry. I say former because the parent company recently bought him out on amicable terms after many years of service. Steve is a fantastic guy, a long-time Torquay local, and owns a couple of houses around town, including the one my family and I usually stay in. It used to be the old Torquay library and there's still heaps of books in there. I must admit I don't read that much, so all those books were never much good to me.

Having said all that, though, I didn't stay there this year, because I would have been there all by myself. Bea was flying out to Italy the following morning on a furniture-hunting trip for her new business, and my stepson Rainer was cruising back on the Goldy with his girlfriend. Instead, I stayed with the Perry family. After dropping my stuff off at their beautiful house and saying hello, I hightailed it down to Bells for a late surf. The surf was tiny, barely a foot, but I paddled out at Rincon anyway. I knew I needed the practice.

I don't know if you've ever been to Bells, but if you're a surfer, or you love the typically rugged Victorian coastline around there, you should see it. Bells is a surfing reserve, and the main break itself is in the middle of a beautiful natural amphitheatre. Looking out from the carpark above you can check out three wave setups — Rincon to the right, the Bells Bowl out front, and Winkipop, which is a fantastic wave, to the left.

That afternoon, while I surfed, there was an awesome sunset. The sky was just on fire. I sat there in the water in front of the big majestic cliff that hangs over Rincon just loving life. I love that big cliff. It's all red and rocky and just seems to have soul. I felt really happy, and glad to be back at Bells. Sadly, it was going to be on my mind all week that that trip might be my last to Bells, at least as a competitor. It's a sad thing to say or think, very sad, but it weighed on my mind all week. Mind you, that's not saying I will retire at the end of the season. I haven't made up my mind yet.

After that beautiful surf I went back to the Perrys', where the whole family was now home. They'd been to an AFL game and their team, the Geelong Cats, had won, so they were all stoked. We all went out to the Surfrider Cafe for a quick dinner, and then came back and crashed out pretty early.

MONDAY 17

WE GOT UP EARLY and went for another surf at Rincon. Again, it was marginal. After that we had to drive back up to Melbourne for the contest press conference. It had always been at Bells before, and they've always had good media and press attention, so

I don't know why we had to go up there this year, but we did. Believe it or not, it was in a shopping mall. We thought we were going there to sign autographs. It was pretty weird, and not really happening. On the way back to Bells I had to do an Oakley promotion. It was a bit of a nothing day.

TUESDAY 18

THE WAVES WERE SUPER-SMALL again so the contest didn't start. I had a little surf here and there while debating whether to go back up to Melbourne again that night for the *Australian Surfing Life* Peer Poll Awards. It was a full black-tie gig, like a ball, and I didn't really want to go. In the back of my mind, though, I knew I more or less had to because I knew I'd won an award. I guess I was always going to go, but it churned in my mind all day.

Maurice Cole came and picked me up and gave me a suit to wear that I'd bought in France about 10 years ago. Maurice used to live in France and I guess I left it at his house; somehow he'd hung on to it. It's a beautiful suit, if not a little bit small. I couldn't really button it up all the way, but I think I looked really good, if I may say so myself. We ended up having a great night. It was a good thing. I accepted my Peer Poll award and thanked my peers mostly, as well as the magazine people. *ASL* is my favourite surfing magazine. They're really beginning to get behind the Aussies and I'm really starting to like the layout of the magazine, and I told them that.

Nick Carroll had taken about an hour to give out awards. He was umming and aahing and making one-minute pauses between sentences in his speech. In complete contrast, Layne Beachley got up to accept her award and she just absolutely raced through her speech. Then I got up and said, 'I don't know much, but I know Layne Beachley could be a race caller and Nick Carroll not!' I guess you had to be there, but everyone cracked up. My award was a framed picture of myself surfing at one of the best places on the Gold Coast, which is called Spot X. It was a beautiful shot, one of my favourites. I was stoked.

We were all expecting the contest to be on the next day because they were expecting swell, so I didn't want to have a late night, but it ended up being just that. Since the function was actually being held at the Crown Casino, before I knew it we were down in the gaming floor and having a good time. I didn't actually gamble that night, but I ended up getting a room for the night there.

WEDNESDAY 19

IT'S NOT REAL SMART waking up in Melbourne when you've presumably got to surf a heat in Bells the same morning, but that's exactly what I had done. I woke up while it was still dark and got a limousine to take me back down to Bells. I'd won the night before, so why not? Luckily enough the contest wasn't on that day. It was still pretty flat.

I slept for most of the day, but when I woke up I learned the swell had picked up. Beau Emerton rang me on my mobile and told me that Rincon was fun so I headed down there for a surf. I chucked my wettie on in the carpark and ran down the stairs. When I was halfway out to the peak, I heard them announce that the Juniors quarter-final was about to paddle out. Spewing. I had just one wave at Bells and then had to paddle over to Winkipop. It was still small, but I had fun.

That night I had to go back out again, this time to the Hall of Fame Awards. It's an annual thing where they present awards for services to surfing and it's held in the Torquay township at the Surfing Australia Museum, just near the Rip Curl superstore. I was to receive an award, but since we still hadn't seen any real waves, I was getting a bit cranky. I was thinking, 'Like, when is this ever going to end, all these awards, and when is there going to be some surfing?' I was not very happy, but I went and accepted my award, as well as being presented with the *Tracks* readers' poll award. That's always an honour, so that was good. Thankfully, it was an early night.

THURSDAY 20

FINALLY THE CONTEST STARTED, although it was really small again. This wasn't the Bells we'd come to know over the years. Like we have in every WCT event, the first round was a three-man heat, and a frustrating one at that. It was at Rincon. I had Corey Lopez and local Torquay and World Qualifying Series (WQS) surfer Troy Brooks.

Like it usually is when the conditions are small, it was a really close heat. Towards the end of it Troy was leading, Corey needed a one-point ride to catch Troy, myself a three-pointer, which is nothing, but scoreable waves were hard to find. Right at the end, Corey picked up the score he needed and won.

Steve Perry's wife, Jo, cooked us a beautiful dinner at home that night. Steve is a vegetarian, so we were eating really nice food all week long. Just as good, it was an early night for a change.

FRIDAY 21

HAVING LOST THE PREVIOUS day, I had to surf what we call the Losers' Round. After the first round of WCTs, the winner goes straight to round three, and therefore has a day off, while second- and third-place-getters from the opening three-man heats are re-seeded for sudden death man-on-man heats. The high seeds draw the low seeds, usually the wildcards, who can never be underestimated, especially if they're locals and therefore know the competition wave well. Such was the case for my draw. I got Troy Brooks, who knows the Bells area like the back of his hand, and is an excellent and smart surfer as well.

We were drawn in the first heat of the day and it was tough. Troy knew how to beat me, by picking the best waves, and well into the heat he had two high-scorers while I was playing catch-up. Things were looking grim. Watching from up in the stands, Luke Egan had a running bet with our Californian mate Pat O'Connell that I could squirm myself out of the situation. The bet was a case of Crown Lager. Pat took the bet, declaring, 'No way!' I used a priority tactic, although I didn't even have priority, and kept him from catching the sets. He only needed a small score too, so I was lucky. Personally, it was a great heat to survive.

I watched a few heats during the day and ended up getting angry because they started using a jet ski to tow people back towards the take-off zone. I am totally against using jet skis in contests, except for rescues or if conditions are massive and dangerous, but this day the surf was only four foot. Their introduction is a new thing by the ASP this year, the idea being to give the spectators more entertainment by eliminating the time wasted by competitors paddling back out after rides. It's especially suited for point breaks, or places like Bells where it can take quite a long time to get out the back. They are supposed to stay right away from the lineup, and they try to, but I think that no matter what, they still put way too much wake into the wave faces. It's just not right.

In my opinion, we are cheapening and defeating our own sport by using jet skis. It's ridiculous. I really look up to those iron man guys. They compete amid a field of superfit athletes, and the man with the most endurance and ocean knowledge is the one who usually wins. I know we're not iron men as such, but then we kind of have to be to win. It's part of the sport, and the use of jet skis is totally taking that aspect away. I don't know how or why, but to me it's just not surfing.

I know that one day I am going to have to leave the pro surfing world. I never want to leave, but if jet skis are to become part of the presentation of our sport, it's one thing I think I'll be glad to leave behind. I sat there at Bells watching guys getting towed out while the next guy on a wave was being stopped from being able to surf properly because he was just dealing with all this wake coming the wrong way in the wave. It travels through your board, especially if you're riding a channel bottom like I have been. I felt like I was the only one noticing it — I was asking people around me, but no one seemed able to see it. I felt like I was in a movie where I was the only one who could see what was happening. I asked some of the judges, and they said they couldn't really notice it. I was thinking, 'Is everyone blind? Am I the only one that can see it?' I could see it as plain as day, and it made me pretty angry.

I watched the defending event champion Shane Dorian lose to Ben Bourgeois that day. In their heat Shane just didn't surf well enough, but my whole mindset was distracted by the jet skis. It made heats a different scenario. The waves simply weren't big enough to use jet skis. It has to be at least eight foot I reckon. Everyone thought it was great, but I just don't like it. Later in the day I went for a surf at Bird Rock, which is along the coast a little back towards town, and it felt good to drop my frustrations and enjoy the waves. That's one of the best things about surfing: the real world and all your cares just float away. I had another quiet night too.

SATURDAY 22

DOWN ON THE BEACH at first light, it was obvious that the swell had risen overnight to about five foot. I went for a surf on my 6'5" channel bottom that I had broken in at Margaret River. It was going so good that, dare I say, I felt untouchable. It was a full moon, though, and the tides were really extreme. The organisers were hesitating about what to do first up. They ended up starting with a few men's heats, then having women's heats. I don't mind watching the girls surf, though a few of the blokes do. Usually the grandstand is clear when the chicks are on.

Women's world champ Layne Beachley got knocked out that morning by Neridah Falconer. Because both Layne and I are world champions this year, and both sponsored by Billabong, people somehow think of us as though we're kind of a team or something. In fact, we're quite different. I don't like to talk about myself at all, but Layne does. Now that may seem a strange thing to say as you sit there reading my words about what *I'm* doing day by day for this book, but you know what I mean. I try to let my surfing do the talking, while Layne is more of a talker and an extrovert. She's the strongest woman surfer, though, and obviously the biggest charger in big waves, and I respect her for that. I like her too, but we really are two completely different people, winning world titles in two totally different tours.

After the end of the women's second round in the afternoon, the organisers decided to go back to round three of the men's competition and announced that my heat would be on late in the day. I was not stoked because I was scheduled to surf against wildcard Mick Fanning in heat eight, and that would put us out there right on high tide, and as I said before, it was a full Easter tide. The heats were going on down at Rincon, but Rincon only handles about three foot, and the swell was about five foot, which is too big for there. It was Easter Saturday though, and there was a big crowd watching and I guess the organisers wanted to keep things rolling for them.

I went up to the contest director and said, 'Come on, you don't have to put us out there. I know I'm the number one seed, and since I've got Mick Fanning it has to be one of the biggest heats of the event. Don't do it! It's not right.' Mick Fanning is, of course, a Rip Curl-sponsored surfer, and it was a Rip Curl event. He lives up on the Gold Coast and I see him surf almost every day. He is a really talented performer. Anyway, the contest director didn't really want to talk about it, saying simply that because of the lack of swell that week, we were running out of time. The whole situation felt like a set up. I couldn't argue, though, and so out we paddled. I still felt confident. I'd been feeling really good all day actually.

So there we were out at Rincon with the jet skis towing us around. I get really amped when I'm paddling back out after a wave, but when you're being towed out on a jet ski sled, you're back out there in less than a minute. That was another drawback I hadn't thought of.

We both got 4's at the start of the heat, and then I think he got an 8.5 and I was like, 'Oh, here we go.' Then I got a pretty good wave and scored 6.5. I had dug a couple of rails and had tried to get close to the crowd, eventually getting some good moves in towards the end of the wave. The inside allowed me to do more but I didn't really get the full potential out of it. They announced that I got a 6.5 as I was being towed back out, but I didn't hear it over the jet ski's motor. That's another drawback of those things.

I thought I could have got a seven-point something, but then again if I hadn't had dig rails, I would have for sure. It was my own fault. Then Mick got a 5.0, and I needed a score of 7.0 or 7.5, so I waited and started really looking for a good wave. With the full tide and swell conditions, though, it was halfway closing out between Rincon and The Bowl, which is the connection point to the real Bells wave and the inside scoring potential. But a good wave did come my way. I saw that wave on the television news that night, and I have to say I think I was underscored. I got some really good turns out of it. I kind of got it wide into Rincon and managed three or four snaps before it doubled up. I then got in a re-entry. I needed a 7.75 and they gave me a 7.5 score. After that I still needed a five-pointer.

I was back out there in a minute with the jet skis, so those things do have one advantage. I picked a wave which I thought was good, but I thought wrong, and it turned into nothing. That was the heat. Full stop, the end of Bells for me. The crowd was really nice, cheering me up the beach, and I acknowledged them. I gave Mick a handshake, and he was understandably stoked, as were the Rip Curl people. For me it was a sad thing.

I didn't leave the beach, but stayed and watched a couple more heats from the Oakley stand. I'm not a sore loser at all, especially after winning the world title. Some people say that I don't try as hard as I did before I won the world title, but I do. In my heat against Mick I was trying really hard, maybe too hard. People think I don't have the will anymore, but I can tell you I do!

Although I lost, I still feel good about the tour. It's only the second event, but I'm loving it, and losing just isn't as painful. Generally, losing is a real painful thing on the circuit. When you're winning you're *so* high, but when you're losing, you're just *so* low. That's a sad part of pro surfing. I think surfing should bring you only happiness because every time you're out there surfing waves, it's a really joyful feeling. Unfortunately, it's a fact of life that if you're competing there are going to be times when you lose.

Losing anything is bad but, like I said, its not as painful as it used to be. Even though I had lost, I was still there hanging with

my friends. I had no intention of leaving Bells, because I love the place so much.

I linked up that afternoon with jockey Damien Oliver. He's one of Australia's best jockeys and, like me, he enjoys having a good time. I met him back in January at the Australian Open tennis in Melbourne, which I had been invited to by Jeff Rafter. Jeff introduced me to his brother Pat and the whole Rafter family, and they took me to the tennis where I then met Damien. He's from Western Australia, but lives in Melbourne now for his job. He's actually a good, confident surfer. Damien is a good friend of Pat's and we all really clicked as friends. Actually, I'd say we're a threesome now; well that's what I'd like to think. They're both great blokes and I love 'em. I think we all love each other's company. There's a certain chemistry there.

Anyway, that night, after I'd been knocked out of the event, Luke Egan, Damien Oliver and myself went out and had a big night at the Offshore Festival, up in the fields behind Torquay. It's a big music concert thing that goes for a few days during the contest. It's a really big event actually; I couldn't believe how many people were there. It was just so packed out! We had backstage passes and so we went in and met heaps of muso types out behind the stage.

Somehow I ended up on stage to introduce one of the bands. I love a microphone, and I'd even say I've got a fantasy about being a rock singer; I just love karaoke. So there I was, in front of thousands and thousands of people, all psyched to sing a song even, but then I forgot the band's name! I couldn't believe it. I just stood there racking my brain, but it wouldn't come. They were called, ummm, Spearhead (yeah, that's right). I just froze, and then this guy stepped up to the microphone and said 'Excuse Mark, he's had a bit too much to drink.' That brought me around, and I snapped 'How do you know I've had too much drink?!' and for some reason everyone started laughing. We had a great night, and then the three of us ended up walking home, at like 2 am in the morning. It was just the longest walk, good but. A nice boys' chat.

EASTER SUNDAY 23

UNBELIEVABLY, THE SURF WAS still small the next morning. I went down to the contest site to collect my prize money, but then didn't feel like hanging around so I split and just hung out. I was feeling a bit lost. I went for a surf at Bird Rock and that was about it for the day's activities.

MONDAY 24

I WOKE UP PRETTY early and went surfing with Damien at Bird Rock, and then went to play golf, but they wouldn't let us on the Torquay golf course because it was too crowded. We walked on anyway, and played about seven holes before it started raining. Damien got a nice birdie actually, after shooting from about 150 metres out of the sandtrap. We then went down to see the contest. It was so hard to watch because the swell had finally risen, a solid six foot, exactly how I like it at Bells. I was sitting there with Jeff Rafter and Damien in the Oakley tent just spinning, going, 'I can't watch this!' Damien said there was a big race meeting on, so we left and went to the pub and watched the races.

ANZAC DAY 25

DAMIEN GOT UP EARLY and went back to Melbourne to go training. He is suspended from racing at the moment but he still has to do his trackwork. As much as I love Bells, I was feeling sad and mixed up so I too packed my bags, drove to Melbourne and checked into the casino. Before Damien left he asked me to ring him if I wanted to go to the races, so I rang him as soon as I checked in. We were going to hang out in the Members' Enclosure, so I needed to wear a suit but obviously didn't have one. I just went straight down to the shops, but they were all closed until 1 pm and we wanted to go to the races at 12.30. You've got to stick to your plans, so I asked the concierge if they would ask for someone to come in early, but they couldn't arrange it. I then waited outside a men's store downstairs for them to open at 1 pm.

With Damien picking me up at 1.15, I was racing around the shop, suits, shirts and shoes flying everywhere. The first suit I saw, I said, 'I'll take that one!' Rather startled, the shop guy was like, 'Do you know how much that is?' It was a Harrods store. He went on to say, 'I think it's about $4000!' I was in a hurry obviously, and just said 'Yeah, it doesn't matter' like I was made of money. I took it and ran out of the shop all dressed up, ready for my rendezvous with Damien.

At the track, Damien took me right through the jockeys' room and then out to meet a couple of the horses that I wanted to bet on. I got to pat them and stuff, just so they'd know I was a nice guy, and worth winning for. A good mate of Damien's had a horse that was racing that day and so I put a few hundred on that, but it didn't win. Then I had a bet on Damien's brother, who was in another race down the coast. I got the good oil on him, but I'd always back an Oliver, Damien or Jason.

As it turned out, Jason got up and I won a fair bit of money, enough to pay for the suit anyway, so it was the best day at the Members' Bar. I blew it on the betting actually. This one horse named Teddy Bear won. I didn't bet on it, but it seemed every chick at Flemington did, and they were all stoked because it paid something like 44–1! Just about every girl that passed us was asking, 'Did you back Teddy Bear?' I wish!

After the last race we cruised with some of the jockey crew for a while and then I went to dinner with Jason and Damien to a nice Chinese restaurant. It was Damien's favourite Chinese place and the food was really good. After that we went up to the Mahogany Room, the high-rollers' favourite room in the Crown Casino.

I had been in there a few months earlier, when I was down for the tennis. I think it was the grand opening. On that occasion I went in with about $800, had half a beer, and lost all my money. Everyone was looking at me weird because I still had my tennis shoes on. In contrast, this time I was wearing a funky suit and I was with Damien Oliver, who is a bit of a celebrity, especially around Melbourne, and I had already won $4000. I was like, 'Let's go!' I was high-rolling and we did well. I won another few thousand playing blackjack. I was being the anchor man to Damien, just making all the right decisions. He was loving me, they were all loving me! We all won some money and had a great time.

WEDNESDAY 26

NOT SURPRISINGLY, WE WOKE up a bit under the weather. I had to get up, check out, and then pay a taxi $50 to lead me in my rental car to the airport. I'm not much good at finding my way around unfamiliar places, especially after a big night. I made it to the plane just in time, and collapsed in my seat looking forward to touching down at Coolangatta. Even though I'd lost my heat, I'd had an absolute ball. I'm planning on doing more of the same for the rest of this year. I still want to win a lot — as many contests as possible — but now the losing isn't hurting as much. I'm feeling good.

As soon as I walked in the door at home, I rang Bea in Italy. She said that things hadn't gone as planned over there with her furniture connections, and that there wasn't a lot happening.

Being back at home without her just wasn't right, so I said, 'I miss you so much, honey. Just come home!' She soon agreed. I told her to pack while I rang our travel agent to arrange it.

I rang Bea back and told her it was all organised. She said she was packed and ready, and would be leaving for the airport any minute. We said our goodbyes and I sat back in my favourite armchair relishing the thought that she and I would be in the same room within 24 hours. I slept like a rock.

THURSDAY 27

I ACTUALLY SLEPT IN for a change, but was awakened quite early anyway by the travel agent. They said Bea had been a no-show for the flight. Qantas had rung them from Rome, saying her Sydney to Gold Coast connection was being cancelled because, according to them, they still had her boarding pass for the domestic leg and so, by their paperwork, she hadn't made the Rome to Sydney flight. I was totally confused because Bea had spoken to me just before she left for Rome's Fiumicino airport.

Instantly, I was really worried that she could have had an accident, or been kidnapped or something. I sat there stressing for hours because, to make matters worse, the airline's computers were down as well. There was no way to check if she was on the flight. Finally the computers came back online and it turned out she was on the flight after all. She had upgraded herself to business class, and so they had cancelled her seat in economy. I was really happy, but exhausted after spending almost the whole day worried.

FRIDAY 28

I PICKED UP BEA from the airport at Coolangatta after a little surf at Kirra. The swell was starting to rise, but clearly I had other more important things to do. It was so good to see Bea, who was really tired after her long flight. We just pretty much talked and stuff all day long, and later went down the Seagulls Leagues Club and got some dinner.

When we got back from the club I switched on *Sports Tonight* for a sec to see if they had had a result down at Bells. Sunny had won. I wasn't very surprised, because he'd already won Bells twice. It seems like he's always in the final there, especially when the contest is transferred down to Johanna (two hours drive WSW of Bells) because of inadequate swell. From the footage on the TV he looked like he was surfing really strong, and the waves looked good too. I think I'd rather him winning it than anyone else. I don't know why. I like Sunny, and I felt it was a good result.

That same afternoon, we were actually supposed to go to Cheyne Horan's wedding on the Gold Coast, but Bea was so jet-lagged we just couldn't do it. I felt pretty bad about not going, because Cheyne has been a close friend for a long, long time, but I'm sure he'd have understood. He knows I wish him and his new wife all the best.

SATURDAY 29

THE SWELL HAD COME up more, and Kirra was quite good, so I was stoked to be back in the water and out there. I surfed several times, although at one stage I was intercepted by one of my golfing mates who is a greenkeeper. He stopped me from going surfing and said, 'Come and play golf!' So I did a U-turn and played golf with the boys. They'd missed me, but probably because they like winning my money off me. We then went to my mate Dickie's house and had a barbie and watched the races, had a few bets, joked, and generally had a good time. I cooked Bea dinner at home later that night. It was a great day.

SUNDAY 30

I FELT GREAT WHEN I woke up with the birds and got back to my standard domestic routine. I went straight to the surf at Kirra and had a ball there for a few hours. For a Sunday it wasn't that crowded. I felt really good, got a few barrels, and it seemed like I surfed really good.

Later in the day, I tried to go to the movies with my stepson Rainer and his girlfriend Chrissy. We hadn't rung up to see what the session times were, though. We checked every theatre in the complex at Coolangatta, but all the movies were well into their programs, so we ended up just going to Hungry Jack's, getting some burgers, and eating them on the beach. After that we went for a walk in the mall. It was nice just to spend time with them anyway. Back at home we got really suburban, and ordered in a pizza for dinner.

may 2000

May

›››› MONDAY 1

KIRRA WAS REALLY good again. I love it when Kirra just keeps on breaking. It's easily one of the world's greatest waves. To that point, on that swell, it had been kind of washy, nowhere near as good as Kirra gets, but it still had some great sections. This day, though, it showed signs of maturity. I had an extra long surf with Luke Egan and Rainer.

Kirra is a full physical workout. If you're lucky enough to survive a wave from the Big Groyne, up the point, all the hollow way through to Little Groyne, down on the north side of Kirra Surf Club, the last thing you feel like doing is paddling back out. Depending on the tide, the rip running against you on the paddle out is absolutely horrendous. Sometimes, well often actually, it's like you're paddling on the spot and getting nowhere. The obvious thing is to get out on the sand, run back around the point to Big Groyne, jump in at the head of the line-up, and try your luck again. I reckon I did the run around about ten times that day.

It was a long way from perfect Kirra, but it was nice and solid. Still stormy, but I like Kirra that way. It was big off Big Groyne, and meaty through Butterbox, which is a section halfway down the point towards that famous hut by the roadside. It was sectiony but good.

After that marathon surf, I basically just chilled at home. Believe it or not, I got right into the domestics, cleaning the house, doing the vacuuming, and I took the washing down to the laundromat. Yes, we do have a washing machine in the Occhilupo household, but I'm no good at it! I can't wash clothes, that is. It's just too easy to take it to the laundromat instead.

Sarge and a mutual friend of Bea's and mine, Ray, came around and I cooked us all a beautiful baked dinner (again, if I may say so myself!). I consider it the best roast dinner I've ever cooked actually. I'll admit I got a few tips at different stages from Bea and Sarge, but it really was a gorgeous meal. After dinner, Sarge and I had a few punts on the dogs, trots, and whatever else was racing on Sky. Sarge played tipster, and although he knows absolutely nothing about dogs or trotters, he tipped me through to a respectable positive margin on my phone TAB account. We backed quite a few winners.

TUESDAY 2

I WOKE UP REALLY early, thinking, presuming, that Kirra was going to be really good. When I first checked it with Rainer, in the pre-dawn light, it looked like there was absolutely no one out. We sat there for a while watching it. It was big. I talked Rainer into coming out with me, and out we went. I thought we were the only two out there, but then Nick Wood appeared.

Nick is a genuine Aussie surfing legend. Since he was 12 years old he'd had all sorts of calls made on him as a future world champ and stuff, but he started so young that by the time he'd reached his early twenties he'd almost had enough of the competition scene. He's originally from Newcastle — his godfather is the great Mark Richards — but now he lives on the Gold Coast, just behind Kirra. I get up as early as it gets, but Nick gets up even earlier. He's often coming in at first light, when the rest of us are checking it. He's a freak. He's a brilliant surfer and a great guy.

So there we were, out in this continually shifting solid line-up. I got one wave that faded out, thereby leaving me in the middle of nowhere, to get cleaned up by a really big set. Still, I managed to get back out. I stayed out for a couple of hours, more so for the training than for surfing. Nick and I did lap after lap, and had some good talks in between. He was looking good, fit as a fiddle, and surfing as solid as ever. I guess we were out there for at least a couple of hours. I eventually went home to wash the dishes and pans from the previous night's dinner, did the vacuuming and stuff, and then took an afternoon siesta. It had been a demanding workout in the morning.

WEDNESDAY 3

AGAIN IT WAS A Kirra day. Rainer and I rendezvoused with Luke Egan at our flat on the headland above Kirra. We walked up past the Big Groyne to Coolangatta Beach to paddle out, and I was about as happy as could be. There's nothing better than surfing with good mates, and Luke and Rainer are two of my favourite people, so say no more.

First up, I caught a wave from Coolangatta to Kirra Beach. That's really, really good. By the time you pull off the wave at Kirra you've got to hope there's a set behind you, because otherwise the rip will take you straight away. The waves were about five foot, and really good. I had a great surf. It was the first day that the swell had dropped and the conditions had improved to a manageable level, and we could actually paddle out at the usual spot beside the groyne. On previous days it had been too dangerous. It was like the raging rapids, but you couldn't even pay for a ride that good: it was better than anything in those American theme parks. They didn't guarantee you wouldn't get killed though. It was just so sketchy.

Halfway through my surf that morning, I took time out to change boards. It was becoming more predictable with the tide, so you could do really good moves, instead of just making a line for a section and pulling in. I went from a 6'6" to a 6'3" channel bottom. I had such a good time, but nothing I got compared to a barrel that Sam Watts got.

Sam is a lifelong Goldy treasure. As a grommet, back in the early 1980s, he was supposed to be the next best thing, but he too bowed out of the scene. A few years back he was Billabong team manager, but now he works for the company that manages Joel Parkinson, Rasta, and Dean Morrison. He's a top bloke, and he loves a good time with the boys.

He pulled into a barrel that morning so skilfully that I honestly thought he was Kelly Slater. The way he manoeuvred his way through it in a way I've rarely seen before. He was brilliant. All up, he had three really good waves. He just went mad. After I'd had enough I waited until he came in, just to say, 'Yeah!' I've got to admit I was plain surfed out after all that, so I just knocked off for the rest of the day and relaxed at home. It was one of those days when you realise that there's nothing better than surfing.

THURSDAY 4

I HAD NO CHOICE but to get up early and go for a surf because Luke Egan and I had to go to a charity luncheon up the coast at Broadbeach. I surfed Kirra, which was pretty decent, but then the Tweed Bar started coming on. It's such a great wave I really wanted to go out, but I couldn't because I had to go home and get ready for the function.

Luke was going to collect me from my place, so I rang to see what car we were going in. He always has a couple on hand — just loves his cars. I'd decided to wear a suit, a really nice black one, to match the car Luke was driving us up in. Later he collected me as planned in his beautiful black HSV Commodore V8, and we cruised up to Broadbeach, rocking up looking pretty cool. The first person I saw when I walked in was ironman Trevor Hendy, and he was wearing a suit too, which made me happy because I felt really overdressed. Suits just don't seem natural on the Gold Coast.

The luncheon was to raise money for a few different cancer charities. I took up a surfboard and they auctioned it off for $1700 which went towards the $24 000 they raised that day. It was a really good presentation because before they got, in turn,

Trevor, Charlie Gilbert, swimming coach Denis Cottrell, and myself up there, they showed a video of each of us, showing our career paths. When it was nearing my turn, I did a little nervous run to the toilet, but when I came out everyone turned around and looked at me. It turned out they were waiting for me. I was like, 'Oops, sorry!'

They had us wired up with remote mikes, but when I went back to where I was sitting to get my jacket, I got in a bit of a tangle. I was putting my jacket on as I hurried up to the stage and the microphone wires got tangled up around my body, so the speaker thing ended up coming out my suit sleeve.

Anyway, I got up there. Former league and rugby great Russell Fairfax was the host and was asking me questions, but every time he asked me something, I had to put my arm and hand up to talk into the microphone and people were just laughing so much. I said to Russ 'This isn't working, is it?' and he proceeded to re-dress me right there on stage. Everyone was just cracking up. Luke said later that he watched two 80-year-old ladies crying with

laughter. It was really funny. We had a really good afternoon and, as I said before, they raised $24 000, so it was good all round.

Everyone went out and kicked on from there, but Luke and I didn't. Luke went home and had a sleep, and I went home and kicked back there. Luke said he went back into Surfers Paradise at midnight and all the people were still there from the charity luncheon. Luke just couldn't believe it. It must have been a big one.

FRIDAY 5

I GOT UP EARLY as usual. It was a bit of a spooky morning, really overcast as it has been a lot lately. None of the assembled surf photographers had been happy with the light. I surfed Duranbah, where I found the banks were really nice, obviously having been rebuilt by that same swell that had broken big for almost a week at Kirra. I had a ball and surfed for about four hours because I'd been putting in about six hours a day at Kirra during that swell. I felt good but tired after the surf, so I treated myself by taking the rest of the day off and just goofed around, watched a few races and stuff. It's good doing nothing sometimes.

SATURDAY 6

BACK AT DURANBAH AGAIN for an early surf. It was really good, clean and offshore as well. I only surfed for about two hours, though, because I had heaps of things to do before leaving for the Gotcha Pro in Tahiti the next day. We'd had a report from the ASP

Tour Manager Peter Whittaker that they were expecting a huge swell over in Tahiti, so I had butterflies before even getting on the plane. The wave we surf in the contest there is radically powerful and dangerous.

SUNDAY 7

LUKE EGAN AND I caught the same flight out of Brisbane late in the morning. As we buckled up for takeoff, Luke said, 'Here we go again, jumping in the deep end!' We looked at each other and both knew we were pretty much freaking. The flight was nice enough, just a short haul. We stopped in New Zealand before arriving at Papeete airport in Tahiti about 1 am. By the time we got the hire car organised we didn't get out to Manoa Droillet's house, where we were staying, until about three in the morning. It had been a long day, yet I found it hard to sleep. It was only a three-hour time difference from home, so the body clock shouldn't have been that out of sync, but I guess it was. I eventually drifted off.

MONDAY 8

WE WOKE UP IN the morning to find the swell huge! The previous year we'd paddled straight out the first morning at Teahupoo, the contest reef, and there had been some solid 12-foot waves. As we paddled into the take-off zone we watched a couple of guys getting rescued. It was heavy. I lost my board first wave and it ended up broken in three pieces. Luke broke his board too.

This year we decided not to do that. We were both quite tired, and since the event wasn't scheduled to start for a couple of days, we just cruised and paddled out later at Taapuna. Ninety-nine percent of the breaks in Tahiti are a couple of hundred metres from shore, out off the breaks in the reefs that edge the lagoons encircling the islands. If you don't have a boat, there's some major paddling involved to get out to the waves. Lucky for us, some guy with a boat gave us a lift out. It only looked about five foot from the shore, but when we got out there it was a solid eight foot and really sketchy. We caught a few and just came in. Both of us looked at each other and said, 'Imagine how big Teahupoo would have been!'

Teahupoo is a township, literally at the end of the road, on the eastern end of the main island, about 75 minutes drive from Papeete, the Tahitian capital. Out off the edge of the lagoon there is one of the most incredible waves in the world. It's a big beautiful peak, but it can show such a mean face. It is so thick that you can't even describe it. It throws the biggest heaviest lips, literally thousands of tons of water straight out of deep water, onto dry reef. It is such a sight. It scares you just looking at it. It has a very distinct shoulder, so you can usually look at it up close and still be safe, but when you have to paddle into its jaws it's another matter. Quite simply, it could kill you. If you're not scared, you're crazy. It would have been almost out of control that afternoon.

We went for a bit of a drive later in the day. Tahiti is one of the most beautiful places in the world. The scenery is just incredible. There we were driving around pretending to be admiring the scenery when, in fact, we just couldn't get Teahupoo off our minds; well, I certainly couldn't get it off my mind. I was thinking,'What happens if I get cleaned up?' You can die out there. We were driving around and I was mulling it over and over in my head, 'This is really heavy, I just hope that we get through it.'

TUESDAY 9

WE GOT UP THE next morning and found the swell had dropped to about six foot, although there were still some bigger ones. I had drawn Andy Irons, who had won the trials the previous day in incredible waves. He was *the* surfer of the contest so far. Some people who'd watched him the previous day were saying he'd done the best backhand surfing they'd ever seen in the trials. I was like, 'Oh great!' 'cause I had him in my heat.

It was like 4–6' for our heat, and he was doing some unbelievable things. I got a couple of barrels, and scored a couple of 7's, but I was never in the game. He had 9's and 9.8, and I think he even had a 10 in the end. I think I was freaking myself out. I was saying to myself, 'Come on, get over it! So I didn't win my heat.' I had to get on top of it, and get back out there. I went to bed pretty early that night, but I remember it started raining really heavily sometime during the night. It was absolutely pelting down — a full tropical downpour.

WEDNESDAY 10 > SATURDAY 13

WE WOKE UP TO the sound of the rain still thundering on the roof. It rained, and it rained, and it rained. The swell had got massive again, so they couldn't have the contest. It was too wet and windy. For two days we just hung out at Manoa's, playing pool and surfing the beach break in front of his place. His home is quite a long drive from Teahupoo, but his family are great and they treat us like long-lost relatives. We love 'em. Shane Dorian and Ross Williams stayed there as well.

One day we went to Teahupoo in the rain and surfed the river. After days of torrential showers the water was cascading down the mountains, which are just a couple of hundred metres from the shore. The river of water that runs off the mountain gorges ends right on the beach. It was unbelievable this day. We were trying to cross the river, and it was like the gnarliest rapids. We'd get on our boards and just go so fast in this raging torrent. We went there several times during those couple of days and mucked around.

SUNDAY 14

FINALLY THE RAIN STOPPED and the morning dawned semi-clear. We drove to Teahupoo to check if it was going to be on. In the early morning light we couldn't see how big it was, but it looked fairly solid. We went out there in a boat with the contest director and the head judge. It was too dangerous to be out there by yourself. The contest director reckoned it looked good, though it had a weird lump to it. It looked about 6–8'. He asked me, 'What do you reckon?'. We went and grabbed our boards, 7' and 7'2", and went back out there. It looked like someone had just turned the volume up to maximum. It was huge, some solid ten-foot sets, and being in the third heat, I was freaking.

Koby Abberton was out there just going mad and charging anything. Andy Irons got the biggest, hugest barrel you could imagine, and had to dive off helplessly inside the thing. It was death-defying. I jumped in and there were like ten guys out there frothing. A big set came and I'm glad to say it wasn't my turn. Soon after they started clearing the water to start the contest as these ten-foot sets were pouring through. I was kind of happy I hadn't caught a wave in the circumstances, but for my efforts I should have at least caught *one* wave. It was a bummer, but it was big and, I'll admit it, I was scared. If I had my time over again, you know how it goes . . .

Just as they were counting down to the start of the first heat of round two — '5,4,3,2,1' — this massive 12-foot solid set came pouring through. Everyone was screaming, 'Watch out!' The bottom of it sucked down below sea level and just pitched like a mountain. It was *so* big and powerful. Competitors Sunny Garcia and Shane Wehner were caught inside where it broke. Sunny threw his board and got sucked down under it, but Shane tried to hold onto his board and got sucked back over the falls with the thing.

I think he maybe got off with a severe pounding, but then the second wave was just as huge and it pounded him down. By that time the set had passed, his board was tombstoning, bobbing up and down vertically, half out of the water on the surface, while he was obviously pinned down underneath at the other end of his leg rope. It was heavy. A jet ski zoomed over and pulled him up by his leash. Meanwhile, we were all sitting there in the channel watching this, going, 'Whoa!' That was how the round started. Sunny took a few big drops but Shane Wehner was obviously shaken up. He got pile-driven into the reef holding his board. Oh my goodness!

The next heat included Taj Burrow and another monster set failed to materialise. I was in the next heat and was thinking that those sets probably came only every hour or so. You're just helpless when you're out there in the wave-catching area, the take-off zone, if a set like that comes. It's gonna get ya! It is just so intimidating and a very uncomfortable feeling when you have to surf a heat in conditions like that. You can paddle way out and get away from it, but then you won't be able to catch a wave. So I caught a few safe waves, a few smaller ones, like 6–8', and got pretty low scores, but enough to beat my opponent. I was pretty happy with that.

Luke surfed later and just went mad. He got some big barrels. It was a really scary day, especially since, just two weeks earlier, a friend of Manoa's had been killed out there duck-diving a rogue set. Something like that could happen so easily to any of us. It turned really big and onshore in the afternoon. Really ugly. I was glad after all that that I'd surfed early before the wind came up.

MONDAY 15

We arrived back at Teahupoo to find the waves had dropped to around the 5–6' mark, and the swell direction wasn't as heavy. I've got to admit to being a bit relieved, for I could now concentrate on surfing rather than survival. We had a surf in the morning before the event started, and it was pretty good. Luke Egan won his heat in awesome form, smoking our mate Taylor Knox. It was a great heat.

My little Narrabeen mate Nathan 'Hog' Hedge had an excellent heat too. He's a WQS surfer who just missed the cut for the top 44 last year. He surfed Sunset incredibly well in the last event of the season, and would have been in the WCTs this year if he'd made it through just one more heat. He got called up into the Tahitian draw when a few guys had to drop out because of injuries. He'll be up there in the top 44 before too long, probably next year. I love little Hedgey. He's a true Aussie ripper.

My round-three heat was the last one of the day. It was actually slated in the draw about four heats earlier but my opponent Andy Irons had been in hospital for a few days with staphylocossus, or 'staph' for short, so the organisers asked if I minded our heat being the last of the day, to give Andy the maximum time available to recover and rebuild his strength. Russell Winter and Richie Lovett also got staph that week. It's a bacterial infection that's supposed to come from reef cuts, and just a little cut can see your whole leg blow up like a balloon. It's radical.

Apparently Andy checked himself out of hospital that afternoon, against his doctor's advice, of course. When he turned up he looked alright. I asked how he felt and he said he felt better than he had, obviously. As he surfed the heat, though, you could tell that he wasn't right on it. He surfed well, but his balance was definitely a bit off. I had some good waves myself and won the heat, finishing with an 8.0. I was stoked with that. Admittedly Andy was handicapped, but still, I'd gotten through a wildcard heat against the toughest wildcard there is.

TUESDAY 16

THE SWELL WAS DOWN a little further again, still averaging 4–5' early, with the odd bigger ones, but it was holding its shape really well and running through extremely clean and hollow all the way to the channel. Teahupoo is such an amazing break. I was drawn in a morning heat against my young mate Beau Emerton, and I couldn't seem to do anything wrong. I got some really nice barrels and scored a couple of nine-pointers. It was great! I rode my 6'6" rounded pin. It's a really nice board and perfectly suited to those conditions and those size waves; it just felt like it was part of me in that heat. I scored 25 out of a possible 30 points, and was really stoked. Luke won his heat in fine style too, after which we went and had a good breakfast and laid around for a little while, before going back for the quarter-finals.

I had Corey Lopez and had another good heat, scoring a 9.0 and an 8.0 among my counting waves. I really admire Beau and Corey and both of those heats were tough, as I knew they would be, but I was feeling good and having fun as well. That means 'relaxed', which is always when I produce my best surfing. Then I had Kelly — and I stopped having fun.

Instead of just surfing as comes naturally, and going with the flow, I tried too hard — I always do against Kelly. Sure enough, Kelly went berserk, as *he* usually does, and won comfortably. He 'comboed' me in fact, which means I needed more than ten points, two wave scores, to catch him. I shouldn't have said it, but at the end of the heat I paddled over to congratulate him and

said, 'It's never going to happen, is it?' meaning I was never going to beat him in a man-on-man heat. We'd surfed against each other something like 10 times, and I'd beaten him in four-man heats, but never to that date man-on-man. It's one of the bugbears of my life. He just smiled and said, 'Well, maybe next week.'

We watched a few of the first waves of the final between Kelly and Shane Dorian, but then collected our prizemoney and left Teahupoo to head back to Manoa's, and started packing. After packing our board bags and thanking Manoa's family for their awesome hospitality, Luke and I had a few cocktails around the pool at The Beachcomber and then went to the airport to check in for our flight. It was a good one because I had three seats to myself all the way home.

WEDNESDAY 17 › SATURDAY 20

AFTER GETTING SOME FAIRLY decent sleep on the overnight flight, I arrived back in Brisbane on the morning of 17 May. Because I had two big board bags, which are like the size of stretched coffins, I hired a station wagon and drove down to the Gold Coast. The weather was gnarly, quite cold, and certainly in complete contrast to the tropical weather we'd just experienced in Tahiti.

I went straight to the Healthy Bee at Kirra for a smoothie, like I always do when I fly in, and then went home. I gave Bea some duty-free perfume and a new wallet, and Rainer a box of chocolates. I guess I'm not that good at picking or giving presents. I went for a surf later in a 4mm steamer, which is unheard of on the Gold Coast. It's the thickness you'd wear in a cold place like Bells or Jeffreys Bay, and even then only when it was extra cold. I just couldn't find my 3mm steamer, though. I do surf in steamers a lot. The waves were about 2–3' and really crappy. It felt weird surfing that after the waves at Teahupoo, and shooting really fast through barrels. I was feeling really quite jet-lagged, so I went to bed early that night.

The next morning I went for a surf with Luke Egan, and again we talked about how weird it felt to be back on small boards surfing little beach breaks. We both felt like we were surfing really slow. I hung out most of that day at home, watching TV. It was pretty much like I was in transit. The Tahitian event had finished four days ahead of the end of its waiting period, and the Quiksilver Pro was scheduled to start three days after that, on 23 May. If Tahiti had used all its waiting period, we would have had just 24 hours at home before flying out to Fiji, but instead we had five days. It was basically five days of slothing.

I went for a surf each day, watched lots of TV from my favourite armchair, and generally just hung out. I didn't even start up or drive my Jeep, but just drove the rental car around. I didn't even take my board bags out of the car, instead I drove around all week with them in the back. I did take my suitcase out of the car, but only to unload the contents at the laundromat. I picked up my laundry on the Friday, chucked it in my bag, and was instantly packed! The night before I flew out Blair, one of my local mates, dropped around to say g'day. We had a couple of quiet beers before dinner. I went to bed early.

SUNDAY 21

I GOT UP A BIT later than normal and went for a little surf, just to get wet. I love to go for a surf before catching a plane. I then went home, threw a 7'6" in one of my board bags, said goodbye to my family, and hit the road for Brisbane airport in my rental car. I was pretty sceptical about going to Fiji. It had been on the news bulletins the previous week that there was a full-on coup taking place over there. A lot of us were worried about flying into the middle of it, but the ASP said everyone was still going, so I went along.

I saw Danny Wills at the airport with his wife and kid. It was his first comeback event after having an ankle injury. I asked him how it was and he said he had only been for one surf. It was good to see him back — he's such a good guy. I really admire his surfing, so fast and really positive. I also really like his approach to a wave. We went up to the Qantas lounge and saw ASP administrator Peter Whittaker and surf photographer Peter Wilson ('Joli') having a chat. We got talking about the coup. We were going anyway, they said, so there wasn't much point being concerned.

It was a short flight from Brisbane to Nadi, only about three hours. It takes the same time to drive from the Gold Coast to Angourie in NSW! We got picked up from the airport by a Quiksilver-organised crew. The whole scene seemed pretty quiet, though it was dark. They'd made an announcement on the plane, telling us not to go out after 10 pm or something, which sounded pretty sketchy, but there we were, safe and sound.

We all checked into the Dominican Motel in Nadi at about 8 pm and had a nice dinner with Willsy and his family and Peter Whittaker. They had cans of VB at the bar in the dining room, which was great. Needless to say, we hung out after dinner and had a few. A lot of crew rocked in quite a bit later from the Sydney flight, including Mick Lowe, South African Greg Emslie, and all the judges. I had previously arranged to meet up with Luke Egan and Matt Hoy that night, but they were on a different flight to me from Sydney. As it turned out, they booked straight into the Sheraton. It was a bit of a late night, and then I couldn't sleep, so I ended up having a sleeping tablet.

MONDAY 22

AFTER A HEALTHY BREAKFAST at the Dominican we jumped on a fleet of mini-buses and headed through the countryside for about 40 minutes having a good chat amongst ourselves. Bus trips are always fun. We heard that there was plenty of swell so we were excited to arrive at the pickup point about five or six kilometres inside the big bay behind Tavarua and Namotu.

It was full-on high tide, and we stepped straight off the land into the boats. Last year we had to walk 100 metres across dry reef to get to the boats. There were even little one-foot waves breaking on the beach there, all the way inside the bay, so we knew there was good swell outside. They ferried us all out there in lots of big whaling-type boats. After five minutes of motoring we saw this huge set on the horizon at Cloudbreak. It was probably about eight kilometres away from where we were, and you just know that when it looks big from that far away, it has to be B-I-G! The closer we got the bigger it got. We were all like, 'Whoa! It's huge!'

As soon as we arrived we were met at the water's edge by Scottie, who is manager and part-owner of the Namotu Island

Surf Resort. He's a really great bloke. Matt and Luke were already out there on Namotu, and so our little group was reunited in the same hut, Burre 1, that we had stayed in the previous year. It was great to get the three of us back together. Last year we stayed together and ended up having a great result, as well as an excellent time. We were obviously hoping for the same this year. At that stage, we didn't have our boards. They were coming on a later boat, so we couldn't get straight out there. We actually had a little snooze until the boards arrived. When they did arrive, we got ready for a surf and headed down to the beach to get a ride out to Cloudbreak on one of the Namotu boats.

Tom Carroll, Taj Burrow and Jake Paterson came in on the same boat that we were waiting for. They reported it was 10–12' and barrelling big-time, going, 'You're gonna freak, you're gonna love it!' They were just charged up. I started to get butterflies in my stomach, thinking to myself, 'Are we ready for it?' Indeed, it was 10–12' and there was a huge clean-up set steaming through just as we pulled up into the line-up. It was the biggest and cleanest Cloudbreak I'd ever seen.

Luke went straight out into it and just got cleaned up inside before getting some really big barrels. I sat a bit outside for about 15 to 20 minutes, sussing it out, not wanting to get cleaned up first thing. My first wave was a big one, like a 10-footer. I didn't get barrelled but I got in a nice big turn and then flicked out. I was on my 7'2" which felt really good. I then got another mushy one before braving it sitting right on the inside. I got cleaned up quite a few times, but ended up getting a couple of smaller inside barrels. Fully churning stand-ups they were. I got out after a couple of hours, while Luke stayed a bit longer and got a few more barrels. It had been like jumping in the deep end straightaway, but it felt good. We then headed back to Namotu for lunch.

It was great to be back on Namotu, which is a beautiful island, not much bigger than a couple of football fields. There were almost a hundred people involved in the Quiksilver Pro — the competitors, judges and event staff, heaps of press and media, plus a huge international contingent from the Quiksilver company, as always, so we were all spread out between the two islands.

Last year Namotu was a full-on Aussie camp, while almost everyone else stayed on Tavarua. This year there were quite a few Aussies on Tavarua, but Namotu was still basically an Aussie stronghold. They have a great bar there, and Scottie is a lot more flexible in his trading hours than the Americans who run Tavarua. I think the food is better on Namotu too. If you want to have fun, you stay on Namotu. Pretty much all the same staff were there as last year — Esther and all the girls who serve our meals, and clean up and stuff — and they seemed stoked that we were back. They were my cheersquad last year, really encouraging, so I was pleased to be back there too and see them all again.

Later that afternoon, we all had to jump in the boats to motor the couple of kilometres over to Tavarua, about a 10-minute ride, to go to the event's opening ceremony. It was a traditional kava ceremony, with all the local tribal chiefs, which are always really good. Kava is the local brew that they all drink. It is made by crushing up a root called kava kava and mixing it with water. It's got some sort of anaesthetic in it, because it kind of makes your mouth and tongue go a bit numb.

We all waxed up and took over our small boards too, because the wave over there that wraps around one side of the island,

Restaurants, was breaking. The way it breaks, it is one of the best waves in the world. It's a really fast and hollow left, and you get more and more speed out there as you go on down the line. It's just amazing! You can get the longest tube rides out there, 10 to 12 seconds, no worries. It gives you so much speed the way it wraps around and draws off the reef. It wraps like a full elbow, through 90 degrees and you actually end up facing back out to sea where you flick out.

We all jumped off the boat as we went past the Restaurants reef and went surfing for about an hour, hoping that the kava ceremony would take a little longer to get started. By the time I got in to shore, it had already begun. Kelly was there as Quiksilver's wildcard. He and Sunny Garcia and myself presented the big chief with some bunches of kava root, as a mark of respect as well as a gesture of appreciation for letting us come.

All the top 44 sat around on the ground on this massive woven straw mat, but we all had trouble concentrating on the ceremony. We all kept looking over our shoulders watching unbelievable waves reeling down the reef at Restaurants. I just couldn't stop watching the waves. It was really starting to pump, and so after the ceremony finished, I went straight back out and caught a few more waves before it got dark. One I got was a really nice barrel. We motored back to Namotu just after sunset and had a few beers and dinner. Everyone was just stoked to be there.

TUESDAY 23

THE FIRST DAY OF the waiting period for the event and, of course, with plenty of swell around we were straight into it. As soon as we woke up, they told us the waves were at least 6–8', with some 8- to 10-footers. We got our boards ready and motored out for an early surf. I got a big barrel. I probably thought it was bigger than it looked, but I didn't really get any big ones the day before, so that barrel felt good and gave me some confidence.

The contest started about 9 am. I caddied for Luke in his heat and watched a few others. Luke was in heat three, surfed well as always, and won his heat catching a really big wave in the process. As he tried to pull into the massive tube, the lip hit him square on the shoulders, but somehow he didn't fall off. He's a strong bugger. He carried on to place himself perfectly in a big, big barrel, a solid 10- to 12-footer!

Tim Curran surfed well that day, as did Mick Campbell, Sunny Garcia and, of course, Quiksilver's other team wildcard, Tom Carroll. I was impressed with Taj Burrow, who won his heat. Mine was the one after his, but the waves were slacking off a bit, perhaps with the tide. I took my 7'0" board out, and I could have maybe taken a smaller one. I actually wanted to swap for a smaller board during the heat, but my best mate and caddy didn't turn up, which is very unusual. Luke is usually Mr Dependable.

As it turned out, he was there sitting on a jet ski with my smaller board, which was totally unexpected. He'd gone back to Namotu for a siesta after his earlier heat and overslept, missing the boat back out to the reef. When he woke up late he'd borrowed a jet ski from the island and ripped out there, and got my spare board off Sarge in one of the photographer's boats. I was looking around at all the caddies and crew sitting in the channel, stressing, wanting to change boards, but couldn't see Luke. It didn't matter really because I didn't win my heat anyway. I was kind of snapping, but after I found he was there after all, I was OK. We went back to Namotu after that and just kicked back for the rest of the day, had some dinner and had a pretty early night, in the knowledge I had to surf in round two the next day.

WEDNESDAY 24

BEING THE HIGHEST SEED to lose in the first round, I was in the first heat of the day against the lowest seed, the local surfer Matia Waqa (pronounced 'Wonga'). He works at Tavarua Island Resort and he's a good surfer but, needless to say, he hasn't got much contest experience, so it was the easiest draw of the round. I slipped into a couple of early waves, and really only had a mediocre heat, but still won convincingly because of my adversary's competitive inexperience.

Actually, I felt it was a great honour to surf out there with just a Fijian brother and myself in the water. It was a very special thing, and I loved it. Waqa's a great guy. In the next heat Tom Carroll beat Jake Paterson after a thrilling exchange. I just loved seeing Tom surf again. We had some great heats in the 1980s when I was a grommet. He hasn't lost any of his power or raw aggressive surfing style. He still has his speed; he hasn't lost an ounce of it. Lots of us were watching him surf, scratching our heads, thinking how incredible it is that his skills haven't deteriorated at all. He's super-fit as always too. We all love him. Tom is a surfing icon.

Young Troy Brooks beat Nathan Webster next in another great heat, and it was looking like we were in for a day of upsets. It was a great day's surfing. The first State of Origin rugby league game was on that night. We all love our rugby league, especially Luke. Namotu has satellite TV so, just like the year before, we gathered around the big screen hooting, hollering and jeering. Strangely there wasn't a Queenslander to be found, which is probably just as well because NSW kicked their butts! Don't ya love it! A couple of the Hawaiians and lots of the Quiksilver staff came over from Tavarua to watch the game too. I heard it ended up a big night, as it always does. I had a couple of beers, but reefed myself away from it and went to bed just after half-time because I knew I had a big day coming up.

THURSDAY 25

We were all surprised as we ate breakfast, stunned even, to find the contest was being put on standby. The swell was still quite large, about 6–8'. Admittedly, it had a wicked wind coming up the face, but the contest director surprised me by calling it off because the waves were still big. I thought that maybe they'd have run with it. It was kind of weird, because when they start calling off the contest like that it can risk or wreck the true end result of the event, but that's obviously got nothing to do with me.

In the afternoon Luke and I went for a surf at Cloudbreak all by ourselves. The wind glassed off, and there were a couple of big barrels. I tried a new board but it didn't go well. It was really slow, so I couldn't even get into that surf at all. I think a little bit of a hangover from the State of Origin showdown might have had something to do with it too. We took it easy that night. I was tentative, but still amping knowing I had a heat coming up against Kelly Slater. Just about more than anything in my life, I had to break that hoodoo of always losing to him.

FRIDAY 26

TODAY TURNED OUT TO be my own 'Good' Friday. I woke up early and went straight out to Cloudbreak in the first Namotu boat. The waves were nice, really clean, and I got a couple of nice tube rides. It was great. I felt nice and comfortable. As we came in, they were clearing the water to start the first heat between C. J. Hobgood and Mick Lowe. Everyone on our boat wanted to bail back to the island though, so we headed back for breakfast.

I remember feeling good about myself as I ate breakfast. I'd already started the day with a good surf, and I felt well prepared for my match-up with Kelly. I was going to catch the next boat back out to the reef, though I did have my reservations about being on the big mother ship for too long before my heat. The Cloudbreak reef is in the middle of nowhere, a few kilometres out towards the open sea from both the Tavarua and Namotu islands, so Quiksilver have to hire a base boat that everyone can hang out on as the daily schedule unfolds. It's a massive two-storey catamaran, called *Island Express.* Shuttle boats then run back and forth from it to the islands every hour or so.

Always out there as well is Quiksilver's *Indies Trader II,* which all the Quiksilver Crossing Expeditions go out on, all the photographers' boats, jet skis, as well as the odd passing yacht, so it's like a freeway out there. The *Island Express* rocks quite a lot and it feels weird rocking back and forth out there before your heat. But usually, especially if I'm up against someone like Kelly, I feel quite anxious and want to get out there as soon as possible. It's the wrong thing to do, though. Calm is a most important asset.

For some reason, I changed my routine that day. I had a little snooze after breakfast and was intending to catch the 10 am boat back out to the reef, but I had a sleep-in and missed that one. I slept till 11 am and woke up thinking, 'That's cool.' I felt real relaxed and there were a few heats to go before mine. In retrospect, it really helped me not watching the earlier heats and getting all flustered. When I eventually got out there, I had a little bit of lunch on the boat, and watched a couple of heats.

Sitting there I was really calm, reassuring myself, 'I feel good, I feel good.' The waves were kind of dropping off a bit and people were talking about the conditions, debating whether they should call it off or not. Once again, that had nothing to do with me, but I wanted to surf. I sat there willing the swell to hold, 'Keep going, keep going.' The organisers weren't asking us, but we learnt later that they were wondering why no one had said anything. No one did though, because the heats were rolling well and the waves were still good. It just wasn't as big as it had been.

I saw Troy Brooks beat Taj Burrow, for the first time ever. They've surfed against each other since being mega-groms, eleven times or something. He was stoked — good on him. Taj was stressed, but I think he has to learn to relax a bit more and not hunt success so anxiously. He is a brilliant surfer, freakish, and there's no doubt he'll one day be a world champ, but he has to let destiny take its course. Relax mate! I also saw Sunny Garcia beat Tom Carroll, and then it was my turn.

Despite having good preparation, I did the usual and started off doing something silly. I took off on a wave and somehow stuck my foot into the wall of the wave as I pulled in. I don't know how or why I did it, but I fell off. I was rolling around underwater, cursing myself, 'You idiot! What are you doing!' After that, Kelly started *paddling me* up the point, like he usually does, and I knew then he was going to start hassling, so I took a smaller wave thinking I should just get away from him. I didn't care if I was left with second priority, but then I fell off in the tube anyway. He then took a wave and fell off as well. I was like 'Wow' because usually if I was to fall off, he'd turn around and get a 9.0. You can't give Kelly Slater an inch.

So we had a bit of a paddle back out for priority and I think they gave it to him, but neither of us was sure. I put my hand up gesturing to the judges to indicate who had priority. There's this nice looking five-foot wave coming at us, I'm looking at Kelly, he's looking at me, and neither of us knows who's got the priority to take the wave. They haven't given it to anyone yet, so Kelly swings, I act like I'm going to swing, he falters and ends up just jumping over the falls, totally wasting the wave. Inside I'm screaming, 'Yes!' and so now I've got priority.

Straightaway another wave rolled through. He looked at me again but I didn't go, and it was the smartest thing I did, because he didn't go either. The next wave was a nice little double-up, and I was like, 'Yes, this is a good one.' I didn't have to do much other than just put my hand in the wall and stall a little, and got a nice tube, then did a turn and got another tube. I ended up scoring an 8.5 and so finally, even though we were well into the heat as far as time was concerned, that was a good start to the heat.

Kelly then had priority and a nice wave came, not a barrelling wave, but one with a good rippable wall on it. He went up to do a big snap right in front of me, and kicked his tail out and blew it. It was totally uncharacteristic of Kelly. I seized on that, feeling well and truly in control of the heat by this stage. I got a small wave next and did heaps of turns but got only like a 5.4 on it, and still he had nothing yet. As I paddled back out he paddled into a wave and got a big barrel. I actually thought he fell off while he was in there, but everyone said that he pushed his way through it. He got an 8.5, and suddenly he was back in the heat as large as life. I heard the score and thought 'Oh no, he's back!' but then I was still pretty calm, because I knew I had control of the heat.

Next he pulled into another sly wave, got deeply barrelled again and got a 7.0. All of a sudden the heat was almost over and it was me who now needed a score. Then, I've got to admit, I was back to stressing. Straightaway I got the feeling I knew all too well, like last week when he kicked me in Tahiti. I was stupid to say to Kelly after our semi-final there, 'It'll never happen, will it?' I kicked myself for saying that, and now here I was in Fiji and the same words echoing through my head. He had said, 'Next week … next week.' I'm sitting out there with two minutes to go in the heat, thinking, 'This is next week!'

I needed a 5.8 and, blow me down, in comes this beautiful wave and sets up for me. It was almost too good to be true. Kelly was looking at it too, but of course, holding priority, I went for it. Instantaneously relaxed, I just turned around knowing the wave would give me the score I needed. I took it slow and got on it. I did one turn and then another turn and stalled a bit, and then pulled in and got a barrel. That was it!

I flicked out and Matt Hoy, who was going caddy for me, was right there. He just smiled and said, 'Yes!'

Still tentative, I asked quietly, 'That's it, eh?'

'Fuck yeah, it's got to be,' he laughed back.

There was still a minute or so to go, and as I paddled back out, I was praying, 'Please God, let me beat him just once!' As I got back out there the hooter went, and the contest commentator announced, 'Mark Occhilupo, you needed a 5.8, and you scored a … [really drawing it out] … 7.5.'

Yeah! I was just totally ecstatic, dumbfounded — every stunned and stoked emotion you want to name. You couldn't have wiped the grin off my face for the rest of the day with a front-end loader. I was just *so* happy.

Damien Hardman surfed next, so I went back onto the *Island*

Express and watched him surf a solid heat against Yuri Sodre, which meant, in turn, that I had Damien in the following fourth round. Dooma surfed great in that heat. Then I watched Luke Egan absolutely wax Brazilian Fabio Gouveia with some unbelievable surfing. Poor Fabio never stood a chance. We all headed back to Namotu then and slipped into a few beers later that night. I shouted everyone beer, and I was even buying people cocktails and bottles of wine later. Everything! I was in a real generous mood, but I was just trying to say that I was happy! I was really happy! There's nothing wrong with sharing your joy with your friends.

SATURDAY 27

WHEN WE WOKE UP it looked like the swell had really dropped, so everyone expected the contest would be back on standby, but it was on, taking us all by surprise. We got caught out a bit really, because it was still 4–6'. I didn't feel too bad, considering I'd consumed a fair bit of booze the previous night presuming, of course, that the contest was going to be off.

Actually, I knew why I didn't feel too bad — I'd had an up and under the night before. I'd gone back to our Burre 1 about 8.30 the previous evening. The light was on, and Luke was reading. I turned the fan on and sat on the edge of my bed feeling a bit seedy. Luke must have looked at me as I started swallowing and draining white, you know, how you do before you're about to throw up?

'Are you alright?' he asked.

I just choked out the words 'I think I'm going to be sick' before I bolted outside and chucked a big vomit. It was radical because I wasn't that out of it, but subconsciously my body must have known that I was going to have to compete the next day. I spewed it all out, and therefore woke up without a *real* hangover.

I went for a quick early surf, got some nice waves, and then watched a few heats. It was gnarly rocking back and forth all day on *Island Express*. Everyone was complaining about the waves too. Corey Lopez and Rob Machado didn't want to go out for their heat because they thought it was too windy, or not big enough, or something. The waves were still a solid 4–5' though, and the contest went on. The organisers wanted us to get down to the end of the fourth round, and we did, leaving just the quarter-finals, semis and final remaining.

I had a solid heat against Dooma. He has been on the scene with me for a big part of my life. Growing up we were rivals, he being from the northern beaches of Sydney and me being from the southern beaches. He used to beat me a lot and he was a deadset competition machine. It seems like he's been on tour forever — well, he has, but for the past few seasons he's been saying he's going to retire. He's been trying to stop for years. It's become a bit of a joke, not that we disrespect him in any way, or want to 'get rid of him'.

Anyway, there we were years and years later in Fiji, pitted against each other, in a contest that he has again said will be his last. I felt weird because I really wanted to win the heat, yet I didn't want to stop his career. I ended up winning the heat anyway, after which I congratulated Damien on his illustrious career, shook his hand and said, 'Mate, you done great!' After two world titles and almost countless contest wins, he'd done it all. He gave me a big smile said, 'I'd much rather lose to you than anyone else.' I was stoked that he said that. Dooma has become a really good friend and I love him.

Later on we had a few beers. He got nice and toasty with Beau Emerton. At one stage there, Beau was ripping Dooma's favourite shirt to bits with his teeth. Yes, his teeth. Beau had lost in a tight heat and I was upset for him because he was one of the best surfers there. He's been charging and surfing really good, but he lost too. It happens. A bit of a bummer, but that's life. So, Dooma and Beau both got blind. So they should! They left the next day and the camp was never the same again.

SUNDAY 28

THE SURF HAD DROPPED right off, as expected, and the event was put on hold, waiting for swell. It was a lazy, cruisy day. As Dooma and Beau and other crew left after losing, Quiksilver kept sending people in, so it soon became crammed on Namotu. No other company does it, but Quiksilver always send heaps of their staff from all around the world to their events. In the end, they outnumber the competitors. It's their right I guess, because it's 'their' contest, but it's weird when you're suddenly hanging with people that you don't really know after having been with tight mates on 'your' island. Still, I was happy. I was in the quarters and stoked that Louie was too, and that our super-caddy Hoyo had stuck it out with us.

may2000

MONDAY 29

AT 7 AM THEY TRIED to restart the contest, but I reckon it was a set-up. They phoned us from Tavarua, saying that the surf was 3–5' and they were ready to go. All the judges and three of the quarter-finalists were on our island, and so out we went. When we arrived, there was no one from Tavarua there and the waves were really flat. Not impressed. We went for a malibu paddle later in the day. Scottie has every imaginable type of surfcraft stashed on that island, from conventional boards to kite surfers. He used to be a good sailboarder — well, he probably still is, actually. Oops.

TUESDAY 30

THEY WEREN'T FOOLING us today. We all stayed in bed until it got too hot to stay there. Another flat day, with little two-foot waves on the lefts opposite Wilkes Pass. We went longboarding and snorkelling. The snorkelling in Fiji is unbelievable. I did it today for the first time and it was *amazing*! So many colours it's outrageous. The colours in the afternoon were outrageous too, a beautiful sunset. I sat there watching it, beer in hand, feeling quite content.

WEDNESDAY 31

NOW I'M STARTING TO get restless. Three days without any decent swell, but one is on the way they reckon. The sole highlight of the day was a game of touch footy with the local Fijians. They're all great footballers, those guys. Some of the crew went fishing too and caught some *mahi mahi*, and we had sushi on the bar at sunset. Beautiful!

june 2000

OCCY

On the way to his second WCT victory for 1999, Occy powers off the top at Cloudbreak in Fiji.

(SEAN DAVEY/ALLSPORT)

Occy remains composed at the foot of a Pipeline monster, a wave considered to be the fiercest break on the surfing planet.

(SARGE)

OCCY

(SEAN DAVEY/ALLSPORT)

Having already claimed the world title, Occy wanted to cement his victory with a win at the Pipe Masters but came up against Kelly Slater, who defeated Occy in the dying seconds of their semi-final. Nevertheless, he achieved his aim.

Occy's wife Beatrice helps him celebrate one of sport's greatest-ever comebacks.

(MTV2)

Choosing the right equipment can be the difference between a contest win and a first-round loss. Occy hard at work in the 'boardroom'.

(SARGE)

Occy has adapted well to life on the Gold Coast, making himself at home in the line-up at spots like Duranbah.

(JOLI)

(PIERRE TOSTEE)

OCCY

Although Occy didn't achieve the result he had hoped for, his performance at the Billabong Pro was regarded as one of the best at the event.

When the Newcastle City Pro is held, the whole city comes alive. Occy receives a warm reception on the beach from spectators and fans.

(SARGE)

(SARGE)

The electric atmosphere at Bells Beach often prompts acts of lunacy. Here some of Occy's most devoted fans go to the extreme.

(SARGE)

(SARGE)

One of the newer locations on the WCT, Teahupoo in Tahiti breaks with awesome power over a shallow and razor-sharp reef.

OCCY

The full rail carve is a trademark Occy manoeuvre which demands respect. Not too many can lay it over like the 'Raging Bull'!

Intense as Teahupoo is, if you can negotiate the challenging take-off you might score the barrel of a lifetime.

(SARGE)

OCCY

Reflecting on a free-surfing session during a break from tour events.

(SARGE)

(SARGE)

(SARGE)

Mates Luke Egan, Matt Hoy and Occy enjoy a beer together (certainly not their last!) to celebrate Luke's win and Hoyo's retirement in Fiji.

The WCT top 44 gather to take part in a *kava* ceremony to herald the beginning of the event.

(SARGE)

Luke and Occy's heat in Fiji will go down in surfing history as one of the all-time greats.

OCCY

(SARGE)

(SARGE)

Occy enjoying his time on beautiful Namotu in Fiji.

(PIERRE TOSTEE)

(PIERRE TOSTEE)

Enjoying the freedom of competitive free-surfing in the Op Pro Boat Trip Challenge in Indonesia, an event which allowed Occy to expand his repertoire by attempting and successfully landing aerials.

Analysing conditions at Jeffreys Bay, South Africa, before another tough heat.

OCCY (OLD)

Jeffreys Bay. A world-class wave which makes for a perfect stage when the world's best surfers converge each year for the Billabong Pro.

Style, power and speed are three qualities that define Occy's surfing. When combined on one of the world's most amazing waves, it makes for excellent viewing.

The conditions at Lacanau and Hossegor in France failed to work in Occy's favour.

(SARGE)

Going into an event as the defending champion carries with it a lot of pressure. Occy dealt with it magnificently at Mundaka, ultimately finishing runner-up.

(SARGE)

Always explosive and unpredictable on a wave, Occy bashes vertically in the final of the Billabong Pro Anglet/Mundaka.

(SARGE)

OCCY

June

›››› THURSDAY 1

FINALLY WE'RE ON. The swell is reported as only about 3–5' but with just two days left in the event's waiting period, we're going anyway. We thought that there had been a bigger swell on the way, but it didn't happen. When we got out there we found it was actually more like 4–6', but the wind was dodgy and kind of across and into the face of the waves. I liked the look of the conditions, though. We were down to the quarters. Todd Prestage and C. J. were in the first one, but the conditions were kind of average, the wind kind of messing things up. Still, we were all in a pretty upbeat mood. Luke and I obviously knew we were going to surf against each other, and Hoyo reckoned he was going to paddle out and caddy for both of us at the same time.

By the time Luke and I paddled across to the line-up for our heat, the waves had gone from quite ordinary to really good. It turned *so* on for us. Mine and Luke's heat was just ridiculous — some of the best waves you could ever see; about 5–6' and perfect, a nice light offshore wind and just flawless barrels. Luke and I were paddling across to the peak, and I was thinking, 'Oh my goodness … this is going to be such a heat!' After it was over, some people were calling it the best heat ever. I don't know, but it sure was incredible. We both got barrelled out of our minds.

Luke started with a quick early one, which gave me priority. I waited for a really good one, but maybe too long, for I ended up taking an ordinary one to start. By mid-heat though, it was all coming at us in a flurry. About halfway through the heat, I got a barrel where I was really, really deep. People could see me in there from the channel, but in on the reef the judges obviously couldn't see how deep I was. I was riding the foam ball, and my board was skitting out and going sideways and stuff, and then it came back to me, and I was back riding the wall again. Then the section ahead of me headed off too fast, but somehow I came out the front, through the curtain, which is a really hard thing to do anyway. I thought I was going to get a 10 for sure, but they only gave me a 7.25.

Towards the end of the heat we were both scoring high eights. Luke got a good one and went into the lead and I needed a big score, like an 8.75 or something. I got it though, a 9.25, and then I went into the lead. I was stoked, but I wasn't stoked for very long. As soon as I flicked off and paddled over the wave, I saw Luke pulling into a wave that looked more like Teahupoo in Tahiti than Cloudbreak. I think he needed a 7.8 or something like that, and there he was standing in the squarest barrel you could ever imagine. As soon as I saw him pull into that barrel, I knew he had the score already.

The most radical thing, though, was that when he came out of the barrel he pulled into another smaller sectiony kind of barrel. I assumed it was a bit of a gamble and thought to myself, 'Shit, maybe if he doesn't come out of this he won't get the score after all.' The judges like you to finish a ride cleanly, and they penalise you if you don't. It was a brave effort, because Luke could have straightened out and got the score comfortably. He doesn't know half measures. I rode it with him, in my head and my soul, for a good five seconds or more, and then he just came flying out with both arms raised in the air. I knew it was a 10. It was obvious. What a heat! I was so stoked for Luke. After that, all I wanted was for him to win the contest.

I kept caddying for Luke. Actually, he had two caddies — Hoyo and me. The water patrol came over on the jet ski and said, 'Come on, you can't have two caddys' and I was like, 'Yeah, right. Bullshit!'

Luke ended up winning his semi-final against Corey Lopez and the wind was starting to glass off again, but then as Luke and Guilherme Herdy paddled out for the final, the wind blew back up again and messed things up a bit.

I was telling Luke what to do, to make sure he got three waves, to try and get barrelled. He got a couple of half barrels and did some good snaps, and just wailed on Herdy Gerdy. I was calling out, 'Consolidate, consolidate!' Luke knows that anyway, obviously, but between me and Hoyo, we weren't going to let him lose that final.

Towards the end of it, the water safety guy, Hawaiian Terry Ahue, put me on the back of his jet ski and said that I could caddy from there. So, as soon as the hooter blew, he whisked me straight over to Luke. When we got to him I jumped off to give Luke a big hug, but he was so stoked and excited he almost drowned me. He held me underwater for like 10 seconds! He was like 'Yeah!' with one arm crossed in the other arm, fist clenched, and was holding me under water at the same time. By the time I got up

I was spluttering and choking and croaking like a frog! He heard me and blurted out, 'Oh shit! Sorry Occ!' through the biggest grin you've ever seen, while I'm spitting out water going, 'Faark Lou, what about me!?' I was half-drowning and half-laughing at the same time.

Anyway, Luke, Hoyo and I all jumped on the back of Terry's jet ski and literally paraded our way to the big mother ship. People were cheering 'Louie!' from all the boats, whistling, hooting … Luke was king! It was classic, a great moment, a great victory. Back on Namotu, Scotty and Mandy were stoked that the trophy had been retained by crew staying on their island. That morning, before we had headed out to Cloudbreak, they'd drawn us aside and said, 'Make sure you bring the trophy back to Burre One' — the hut that Luke and Matt and I were staying in, just like last year when I won the contest. It was a perfect day.

FRIDAY 2

WE WOKE UP THE morning after the contest finished, and started the day toasting a beautiful dawn with beers. Don't ask me why. Shit happens. I actually fell asleep early the night before. I was already drained from the excitement and drama of the day by the time we went over to Tavarua for the award ceremony. It's history now what Luke did at the ceremony, where he dedicated his win to our retiring mate Matt Hoy and presented the trophy to him. Everyone was emotional, everyone had a tear in their eye. It was one of the most moving moments in the history of pro surfing. Strewth, we're going to miss Hoyo!

A short time later the guy who runs Tavarua, John Rosemond, went around and gave everyone tequila shots. He gave me a big one. By the time I got back on the boat to go back to Namotu, I was pretty drunk. After we got back there, I think I had one of those skulldrag cocktail things that Hoyo was so fond of last year, and after 7.30 at night I can't remember much. I was that emotionally drained and so stoked with Luke winning that my mind blanked out. You get that!

I woke up early in the morning, about 5 am, and wondered how I had got to bed the night before. Don't you hate that feeling? I wasn't hungover or anything. When the others stirred the first thing I asked everyone was, 'What happened? Did I do anything wrong?' They said, 'No, you were just gone.'

At 6 am Hoyo arrived at the door of our burre with three beers in hand. It's something that I've never done before. Admittedly, I've had many a big night but I haven't ever woken up and grabbed a beer. Personally, I consider Fiji Bitter hard to take at the best of times and at sunrise it was very, very hard to take, but Louie drank his, I drank mine, and Hoyo drank his. Then we just started laughing hysterically. We must have woken up half the camp, but then maybe not. Everyone would have been severely crashed and hungover. Luke's win was so popular that basically everyone had gone bananas the night before. After we stopped laughing, we had a good boys' chat about the contest and other stuff, and then I fell back asleep for a little while.

When we eventually resurfaced, the day's primary activity was packing. After we woke up, packed, and had lunch, with beers again, then we had a few beers more, and then about 4 pm the *Island Express* came to take us back to the mainland. Meanwhile, all day long, we'd heard that Cloudbreak was absolutely perfect. We knew it'd be pissing off a lot of photographers out there shooting waiting for us to paddle out, but we didn't care. I'd had it so good in my heat with Luke the day before that I was already fully satisfied. On my last wave I was in the barrel looking out at Luke paddling out, just pumping away in there, locked in the barrel. Then when I flicked out of that wave and was paddling back out myself, I saw Luke get that incredible 10-point ride. I just didn't want to wreck that image.

Anyway, we jumped on the *Island Express* with all our boards, bags and stuff. I'll readily admit I had a bit of a beer buzz going. We first cruised over to Tavarua to pick more people up and we had to wait a while for them to be brought out to the mother ship. Meanwhile, Restaurants was just reeling down the reef. Mind you, it was only one foot, but in my state it looked just great. I think I was tripping, but I ran down to the next level where all our boards and bags were, grabbed one of the local Fijian's boards and paddled over there. I caught a little wave, just for the novelty of it, then a passing speedboat gave me a lift back to the big boat. On the way the guy driving asked me if I wanted to rope it, you know, what do they call it ... wake boarding. I grabbed the rope, but I couldn't get up at all at first. He was just laughing at me, along with everyone else on the *Island Express*. It took me like four attempts to get up, and when I finally did get up, he was going so fast through a turn that I fell flat on my face.

We then left Tavarua, more beers en route, and headed back towards Nadi where we booked into the local Sheraton. Hoyo and Luke and myself went out for a beautiful Japanese dinner in the Sheraton complex. The food was just so good. We washed it down

with a couple of good bottles of wine too. By that stage we were really smashed, so we went back to our rooms and crashed out.

SATURDAY 3

We woke up very early to check out and catch a flight back home. With all the political unrest, we were a bit worried about what was going on at the airport, so we left extra early. We tried to wake Hoyo up, but he wouldn't answer his phone. He's definitely not a morning person. We banged on his door, and still he didn't stir, so we couldn't do anything about it. Luke and I just left, leaving Hoyo to survive for himself. The airport was packed, but mellow. There were a couple of guys with machine guns at the entrance to the airport, but that was it.

All the way back to Sydney I wanted to sleep, but I couldn't because I was worried about Hoyo. We rang him from the terminal after we touched down, and he said it was fine. He didn't care that he'd missed the flight. Luke and I went to the Qantas club and tried to find a shot of Louie in the newspaper but couldn't find one. Then we jumped on our flight to the Gold Coast. Luke was having a big celebration dinner party that night at a restaurant in Burleigh Heads. We were both pretty excited to get home, and had a beer on the flight to celebrate. Unfortunately, I had to tell Luke that I couldn't come to his party that night. I was only going to be home for one day before having to head off to Sumatra for the Op Pro Boat Trip Challenge. Needless to say, I wanted to spend that time with Bea. Luke was cool.

SUNDAY 4

I HAD A CHANCE TO catch an early surf at Duranbah with Rainer. There were good waves, but it was only small, and it was really cold. I flew out to Singapore in business class for a change, and met up with boat skipper Martin Daly. Arrived there about 10 pm and I saw Mark Richards, who was a judge for the boat-based contest, and photographer Pierre Tostee at the airport. Pierre and Martin and I booked into the Sheraton downtown. We had to stay there one night before travelling onwards to collect our boat. Martin and I had a chat over just one beer at the hotel bar, before we went to bed feeling rather zoned.

Martin seemed kind of worried about what we were going to do and where we were going to go. As the original explorer who opened up Sumatra as a surfing destination, I guess he wasn't that comfortable with taking a four-boat convoy to too many secret spots, and yet the whole expedition was costing megabucks, so they had to get waves to make it pay. It had been seven years since I was last in Sumatra, so I was looking forward to the adventure.

Later, after the others had gone to bed, I couldn't really sleep, so I was watching a bit of TV. Suddenly the bed started rocking. It was an earthquake! All the other surfers and crew for the trip were already down in Padang, and they all felt it too, but much more radically. They all ran out of their hotels because the whole place was shaking really badly. I was just lying in bed thinking, 'Geez, I haven't had that many beers, and I'm not on the boat yet …' I couldn't work it out, so I just rolled over and finally went to sleep.

MONDAY 5

I WOKE UP AND FELT like going for a surf, but obviously there's not much in the way of waves in Singapore. I wasn't flying out until lunchtime, and I was bored. I went downstairs to the gym, which I rarely do. I was running on the treadmill while looking up at the news on the TV, and they were talking about the earthquake. I was like, 'No way! I felt it!' It tripped me out.

After breakfast with Martin we bundled up our stuff and went to the airport to jump on the plane to Padang. The flight was packed with so many people, including many surfers heading for Sumatra that weren't involved in what we were doing. There was a pack of Brazilians, and another of Americans. It's just Surfing Central there now.

To be blatantly honest, I really had my reservations about the whole thing, and wasn't really looking forward to it. It ended up being OK though. When we got to Padang it was just mayhem, bags and boards flying everywhere. It's just a little Third World airport. I saw Mark 'MR' Richards again in the 'terminal'. No disrespect intended, of course, but although MR is one of the greatest surfers who ever lived, he can be a bit of an old woman sometimes.

Luke had told me in Fiji how paranoid MR was about catching malaria on this trip. As a family man and businessman now, this trip was a big flashback, a big adventure. I swear, in the terminal I saw him looking around seeing if he could see any mosquitoes. He had his socks on and pulled up, long pants and the only part of him uncovered was his forearms. I saw him slip this spray on just to cover up his exposed bits of skin. I was thinking, 'Oh no, if he thinks he's worried now, he ain't seen nothing yet!'

We eventually got our bags and then I went to go and change some money. I forgot how bad the Indonesian exchange rate was these days and changed AUD$300. I got the biggest block of Rupiah I've ever seen. I thought they'd made a mistake. I was tripping out. We got to the hotel about 2 pm and they gave us a briefing on the contest, telling us what was going on. We put our bags in storage and waited around till buses came and took us to the boat.

When we got to the boat we found that some of the crew had already left, really early. They put us on a boat called *Mangalui*, but neither Shane Beschen nor Sunny Garcia liked it, and for good reason. Six of us were all supposed to sleep in the same quarters, in one big room, and it kind of looked tight with all the bags. Everyone was totally over it before we even left the dock and wanted to get off, although it ended up being the best boat.

It all looked really sketchy at that stage. They radioed Martin Daly, and he said 'Yeah, whatever' but you could tell he had the shits with it, because everything had been carefully pre-arranged. Anyway they kind of hassled us into going with it in the meantime. We had to bail, because our boat was slow. I didn't mind the arrangements at all, and if Sunny, Shane, Bruce, Andy Irons and Tim Curran all wanted to get off, that was their choice. I was happy.

So we left the dock and away we went, with an Aussie skipper and an Aussie first mate. It was night before long, the sea was pretty calm, and after dinner I nodded off. I love sleeping on boats. I don't get seasick at all, and I love the rolling of the boat. It puts me to sleep.

TUESDAY 6

WHEN I WOKE UP we were still in the middle of nowhere. Our boat was really slow. We still had a couple of hours sailing until we got there, wherever that was. I was sitting on the top of the boat. I'd found a nice spot to sit and was quite happy as we chugged along towards the horizon.

Late in the morning we eventually came to a reef called Bank Vaults. The waves were small, like 3–4', a weird fast right. We all jumped off and had a surf. There were a couple of guys surfing there already, but they got out as we got in. It was good, uncrowded obviously, and I had a pretty OK surf and got one decent barrel. However, it was nothing compared to what was coming.

After the surf we had lunch, and then whacked *Braveheart* into the VCR. It became like the hit movie of the trip, and we all started imitating Mel Gibson's key lines. Sunny Garcia was really funny, saying, 'Come here, laddy, I've come to take you home!' with a classic Hawaiian-Scottish accent. After watching Mel, we went for another surf, but it was kind of ordinary in the afternoon, onshore too. Two of the other boats arrived, then we had a short surf a little down the line from there. We all then headed off to a little anchorage led by this little boat called *Foxy Lady*. For the rest of the trip everywhere we went, all the boats went, so it was like our own marine convoy.

I went to sleep early because I was really tired, but apparently during the night there was a rather savage storm. We heard about it the next day when the captains from all the boats got together on our boat and had a good chinwag about it, getting pretty drunk in the process. Apparently it was complete havoc with superstrong winds. At the height of the storm one of the biggest boats, *Indies Trader*, lost its anchor and ended up on the reef. I was told it was mayhem and everyone was stressing big time. Their propeller was damaged, and a hole opened up in the boat. MR was on that boat and he must have been pretty scared because, at one stage, they thought they were going to have to abandon ship! In the end it was OK though, because they didn't take too much water.

WEDNESDAY 7

THE NEXT MORNING SOMEONE put scuba gear on and dived under the boat to inspect the damage, eventually fixing the hole with quick-dry fibreglass. They then motored onwards on one prop, ordering another one to be delivered en route later that week.

The funny thing was that the previous day, when all the boys were spewing about the boat we were on, the cramped quarters and all, the boat we were intending to commandeer was the one that ended up on the reef. The boys reckoned the six surfers were going to kick the other people off their boat and get on it. If we were on it, we would have got the blame for the boat ending up on the reef, as well as had the shit scared out of us. Even at that point, the night before the storm, the boys were still intent on swapping over to that boat. The next morning though, we were like, 'Oh yeah, it's cool, we don't want to go on your boat anymore. It's fine.' It was pretty classic.

So that morning we surfed Bank Vaults again. It was a bit bigger than the previous day, but it was still weird. It was kind of grey and overcast too. Later on we surfed a little spot where the judges and officials had been surfing, down the line a bit. I surfed with Andy Irons, which was kind of fun. He is such a good surfer — a freak. He was pulling aerials every second section, and I managed a couple of 360 reversals. It was a cruisy day. We stayed at the same anchorage as the previous night, and I hit the sack fairly early.

THURSDAY 8

WE MOTORED OFF EARLY to a place called Burger World, a long right-hander with a beautiful backdrop of hundreds and hundreds of palm trees. We surfed all day. It was funny because the day before we had hamburgers for lunch. We were all psyching for this legendary wave called Macaronis, so naturally we all wanted to eat macaroni for lunch. Sadly, it didn't happen.

Burger World was good. Sunny was taking these fat burners, these new pills that he says give you heaps of energy and let you stay out surfing for like seven hours. They were radical. I surfed in the morning in the brightest green shorts you've ever seen. That night, at some hour, we upped anchor and steamed off for another bay. It took most of the night to get there.

FRIDAY 9

WE WOKE UP TO an absolutely beautiful morning. Tim Curran and I surfed this little left called Two Rocks. All the cameras were filming us, and I snapped some of my fins out. It was a weird wave, so fast that it was really hard to get a turn in. On one wave, I did one really fast turn and then another one, but my board felt really weird. When I flicked out, I turned my board over and discovered I had only one fin. One of my plugs had popped out, so I had to go and change boards. When I came back, I found that the second board was better anyway. I got a couple of fast ones, and got some nice turns in. All the other boys were around the other side of this little peninsula. We could see them through the palm trees, surfing rights that were wrapping down the line in front of us. They were boosting the biggest airs, 360 airs too. It looked great from our angle.

After we had lunch the boys were calling, 'C'mon Occy, come surf this right. It's so good for backhand airs.' I don't really do airs. I've never been any good at them, but I went in anyway. They were telling me what to do, and how to do it. For the first couple of attempts, I only got about two inches out of the water, and I'm sure I was looking really weird. Finally I got this nice little wave, got in a nice snap, and then got the perfect section and actually did an aerial. I was stoked!

Every night we'd watch the video footage of our surfing each day, and so we did the same that night. I saw myself do an aerial and I was even more stoked! It was a great day for me because I learnt something new, from Bruce Irons mainly. He was telling me just to tilt my board in, and not do a bottom turn. I was just stoking, thinking, 'This is unreal!' I'd learned heaps in only four days. It was like I was a grommet again. I wanted to catch every little wave that came through.

SATURDAY 10

WE GOT TO A RATHER famous wave call Lances in the morning, and the waves were good. The girls surfed the left. Did I mention the girls yet? They were part of the contest too. Needless to say they had their own division. The lefts were fun at about 3–4', but by lunchtime the boys were over it and wanted to surf the rights. We went over there and surfed it, but it wasn't exactly happening. We were still waiting for meaningful swell, and hadn't had a round of the contest yet. It was better that afternoon. We were on hold to have a round of the Op Pro Boat Trip Challenge, but we had an expression session instead.

SUNDAY 11

WE WENT STRAIGHT TO the Lances left. It was good value, and so it was decided we'd have our first round of the event. It was hard, but it was really rippable. Bruce Irons was doing some really nice backhand airs, and his brother Andy as well. Shane Beschen and Sunny were absolutely ripping it.

Apparently the main reason they wanted to have a round was because they were having this giant weenie roast back in America, their equivalent of a sausage sizzle. Op had apparently arranged the roast in California and had a big screen up there. They were beaming footage back via satellite. It was hilarious. Whenever a big set came, we'd all scream, 'This is going all the way to the weenie roast!' Every time I got a set and someone yelled that out, I just couldn't surf. I was laughing too hard.

I think I came second to Sunny. Sunny definitely won the round but, at that stage, we kind of realised that the judges and stuff really didn't have a clue what they were doing. That evening all the boys got together to discuss some tactics. If the judges didn't really know what they were doing we weren't going to get an accurate result, so we unanimously decided to just split the prize money evenly, and everyone would get the same money. Cutting US$65 000 between the six of us, it basically worked out that we'd roughly get the same as you would winning a WCT, and the winner would get an extra $5000. We were getting along well and we all signed a piece of paper agreeing to it, so that was cool. We also decided that we wouldn't tell anyone about our agreement. Outside of us, the surfers, the only people who knew about it were journalist Matt George, who was on our boat with us, and surfer Rochelle Ballard, who just happened to be on the boat when we made the agreement.

MONDAY 12

WE WERE BACK AT Lances rights first thing in the morning. It was a really nice 3–4'. One of the first out there was Albert, an Aussie bloke who lives in Bali and has a Balinese wife and kid. He has been skippering boats around Indo waters for years, and was vice-captain of one of the other boats in our convoy. Albert is a great guy, and he was catching some really nice waves. While everyone else was prepared to wait for the tide, Albert was making me envious, so I jumped out there early, and it could have been a big mistake.

I paddled over to the reef on my 6'3" Dahlberg which I'd been riding every day and it was going really well. After a few nice little tubes I got this set wave that was slightly bigger than the others, maybe four foot. Out at Lances you've just got no option but to pull in, because if you don't, the whitewater will grab you and you'll end up on dry reef, which is really sharp and dangerous. On that wave I didn't pull in because I thought I was too deep. Everyone later said I should have pulled in and that I would have made the barrel, but I didn't. It was really shallow, so I jumped off and hit my elbow on the reef really hard. I thought I had badly cut myself up but I hadn't at all, which was really good, and really lucky. Geez it hurt, though.

Bruce Irons went out then, and was ripping so heavily. I saw him do a 20-foot aerial and land it backwards and then go into a reverse. It was absolutely unbelievable! The guy is a freak — just so talented and committed. The wave was getting better with every set, so then the comp organisers decided to hold the women's second round. They didn't get it going till 2.30 pm and by then the waves were pumping. It was six foot and the chicks were taking some mean wipeouts, but they were doing well too, starting to pull into barrels. It was so good we all wanted to go out, but they had a two-hour final. We were told that the next day was going to be eight foot, so we let them have it.

When the chicks were done we all went out for a surf and it was pumping really good. After my wipeout that morning I was a bit reserved at first. I'd also had a couple of beers while watching the girls, but it looked so perfect I just had to go out. I was kind of loose with a couple of beers aboard but the one wave I remember was a really good one. I got a really deep tube where I just had to pump and pump in the barrel. I don't want to rave, but I was so in there that I couldn't even see the opening at the end of the barrel, but somehow I eventually came flying out. *Whooah*, what a wave! I had to go in after that, just had to. Sunny, Andy and Bruce were getting crazy mad barrels. It was just going berserk. After we anchored that night, we were all super excited about what the next day promised.

TUESDAY 13

WHAT A LETDOWN! We woke up and found it was onshore. Spewing. Mother Nature is a surfer's biggest blessing, but sometimes the biggest curse. We're at the mercy of the elements in everything we do. We waited there all day, willing and hoping the wind would change, but it just didn't turn. We ended up having an onshore surf in the afternoon, and that was kind of heavy. That night we steamed off to Macaronis. I was feeling quite excited because my birthday was coming up in a few days. I was hoping in advance that I might be able to not just win the contest, but win it on my birthday.

WEDNESDAY 14

WE WOKE UP ANCHORED next to Maccas and looked out the porthole to see nice 3–4' waves. It certainly looked fun, and was quite contestable, so we decided to have a round of the event.

I had a good surf and landed a couple of aerials. The heat was a three-hour session. Sunny wanted three hours — he had his fat-burner energy tablets and he was out there. I was fairly tired by the third hour, but I think I ended up winning that session anyway. It really was a great day.

We anchored for the night in the bay at Macaronis. At most other breaks we usually had to motor about 30 minutes away to a safe anchorage, but at Maccas you can just camp right there. It's a really nice place. I hadn't been there for seven years and it was radical to see how the waterline had risen from the last time I was there. Some of the fringing palm trees were dead because of the rising water. I noticed how much the place had changed, and spoke at length to some of the boat captains about it.

THURSDAY 15

WE WOKE TO FIND that the swell had finally come up. Maccas was a solid six foot, and there were some bigger ones. It was pretty solid, but the wind was a bit weird. Like at home, I'm always up early no matter where I am, and Shane Beschen is the same. While the others slept in, we snuck out for a surf. I rode a 6'6". Besch got a couple of nice big backhand barrels, and I got a couple of nice big drops myself.

Next, there was a big commotion after one of the workers paddled over to announce that the organisers had decided we were going to Raggs rights, and that it would be a solid eight foot. We were told we had to get out of the water and get back on the boat. As we were being told that, the wind was turning and it was beginning to glass off. In a matter of minutes the waves were perfect, and they wanted us to paddle away?! You don't leave perfect waves! I protested, but it fell on deaf ears. We were ordered back on the boat and away we sailed, leaving a perfect and unmanned six-foot Macaronis line-up behind. It was criminal!

It took us about three hours to get there, and we were going over the hugest swells, through big troughs and up over some big, big 15–20' swells. I was asking, 'How big is this place going to be?' Everyone was breaking out their gun boards, getting ready for big-wave surf, but when we got there we found it wasn't any good. It was only about 2–3', and the swell wasn't even hitting it right. We were all going, 'What?!' We were spewing because we'd basically wasted the whole day, and that perfect surf back at Macaronis.

Besch went for a surf out, but the rest of us just put *Braveheart* back on and watched it again, thinking we didn't have time to get back to Macaronis. Well, perhaps we could have in *Foxy Lady*, but it would have been a really rough trip. After a horrifying adventure off the Hawaiian islands years back, which I'll share in my autobiography, I have a phobia about small boats flipping, so we didn't go. We eventually headed back to Macaronis and to dampen our frustrated spirits even further, it started raining on the trip back.

We had a few beers that afternoon. Since it was my birthday the next day and we were going to Macaronis and there was heaps of swell around, I was stoked anticipating that I was probably in for an all-time birthday. We took anchorage just before dark about halfway back to Maccas.

FRIDAY 16

I WOKE UP ALL stoked in the morning to find we were already steaming, and about two hours from Maccas. As we came into the bay, we found all these pieces of wood floating in the water. An Indo boat had gone up on the reef the previous night. Half of it was still there. Heavy. We wondered if any poor buggers had drowned.

We pulled into Maccas to find it was 4–6' and perfect. Happy Birthday! I was grinning so broadly my ears were cracking. It had dropped a little bit but it was still just so perfect. Martin Daly is a veteran of the area — in fact he put it on the map — and he was calling it the best Maccas he'd ever seen. We were obviously going to have a heat.

Every time we had a heat, which we did that day, we'd draw numbers out of a hat to see who would have priority. This time, though, they gave me priority because it was my birthday. I was stoked, and got some really nice barrels. It was a classic. I had all these birthday waves come to me. I was getting weird bends down the end of the line, and just getting so barrelled. It was unreal. I came second to Bruce and was stoked with that. It was such a solid session.

We had a really good lunch. The chef cooked me up a special meal, again because it was my birthday. They really looked after me. The women surfers brought over two huge chocolate cakes after lunch. It was so funny because, as it turned out, Tim Curran got the biggest piece. Tim is a really nice guy, a great surfer, and a Christian, so he can be kind of conservative. So, for a joke, just as he was finishing the cake, pretending I had just noticed him eating it, I said, 'Tim! Tim! There's marijuana in that cake!' Needless to say, there wasn't, but you should have seen the look on his face. We never told him either, that there wasn't any in there. That night Besch reckoned that Tim thought he was stoned because he was convinced that he'd had some marijuana. He had a good time anyway.

In the afternoon we caught a wave or two, and then stopped by the boat and had a beer, and went back out again. I remember after Martin gave me a beer I got one of my better waves, a good barrel, came out of it, and then it had a big section on the end. It was radical. Once again, because it was my birthday, we had a really nice dinner that night, a roast. We sat up on the deck chowing down. Everyone was stoked. By coming second that day, the third round of the event, I had moved into the points lead, so I just don't think I could have had a better birthday. We motored off back to Lances later that night.

SATURDAY 17

WE ARRIVED BACK AT Lances early in the morning to find the wind was totally wrong. We had just one day left in the event's waiting period and we still had a round to go, preferably in rights. That's why we came back to Lances. The wind just didn't swing, though. We sat there all day waiting for it to change, but it didn't seem too interested in co-operating. It was so boring. Mind you, I was kind of happy that it was lousy because I had a hangover from my birthday. I slept most of the day.

Suddenly, real late, about 4 pm, it glassed off and they announced that we were having our round. The waves were pretty sick, and it got really good right on dark. Sunny was ripping and Bruce was getting some wicked tubes. I got a couple of good turns in some waves with wall, and then one barrel. I came third, which was enough to let me win overall. I'd only needed to get fifth or better.

Everyone congregated on our boat for the awards ceremony. They had the women's presentations first. Rochelle Ballard had won. As you'll recall, she had earlier witnessed our pact to split the prize money. She had kept our confidence, not telling anyone of our agreement, so we were all stoked to hear that she had decided to do the same with the women's purse. We all thought that was really cool of her. When it was time for us to get up on the stage, I announced that we had all had a great time, experienced great camaraderie, and that we too were splitting the prize money. I was presented with a nice big trophy, which the organisers promised to send to me back home. So, at 6 pm that night, on the last day of the waiting period, the contest was all over. Contest director Bernie Baker had been freaking, but we'd pulled it off. It seemed bizarre that it was over and we were leaving. The swell was up, it was just so glassy, and it was a full moon, but we were out of there. So often it happens like that. We all sat up on the top deck that night, sipping on a few beers, lamenting that we were leaving. We'd all had enough, though. It was time to move on.

SUNDAY 18

IT WAS GOOD TO be back on dry land and not eternally rocking with the boat. We had arrived back in Padang Harbour early in the morning, and I booked straight into a five-star hotel. First stop was the bathroom for a nice long hot shower. Needless to say, there hadn't been a hot shower on the boat, so it was a deadset treat to just hang out under the hot water, even if it felt like I was still on the boat. When you've been on a boat for a couple of weeks, you seem to keep rocking for at least a day. I was rocking for ages.

After a shower, I settled back to indulge in another part of domestic life that I'd missed — TV. To my surprise, I found a telecast of an AFL game. I'm not into Aussie rules football at all, but it was better than nothing. We all had some beers at the bar later in the day, and then ended up at some Indonesian disco. I think I got up and sung karaoke to some Indo songs, which must have looked and sounded pretty weird. It's just another way of unwinding, though, which is important after trips on boats and when contests conclude. We had a good fun time in Padang.

MONDAY 19

I WANTED TO HEAD back home but, believe it or not, I had to fly out of Padang to Singapore and then to Paris for a press conference! It was cool, though. The press conference was to announce the Billabong Pro Anglet/Mundaka which is a WCT held in early September. It's a great contest, which I won last year by the way, based at Anglet which is just north of Biarritz right down the bottom of the French south coast. When the swell gets big there, we move down the coast into the Basque country of north-east Spain to a beautiful town and awesome left-hand wave called Mundaka.

It's organised and sponsored by Billabong Europe, which is run by two Aussies, Derek O'Neill and Reid Pinder. They're great guys and great hosts, as well as good friends of mine, so I didn't mind helping them out, even if it was a bit of a mission. They booked me business class, though, so that made it more bearable.

I actually overslept in Padang, managed a hurried breakfast, and then beat it for the airport for a midday flight. Connecting in Singapore I then zoned in and out of restless sleep up on the business class upper deck, all the way to Paris. It was a pretty reasonable flight, actually. Business class really takes the edge off it.

TUESDAY 20

THE BIG FLYING KANGAROO touched down in Paris at about six in the morning. Billabong Europe's Team and Event Coordinator

Carl Wieser met me at the Charles de Gaulle airport. We jumped in a taxi and got stuck in the most radical peak-hour traffic. You're sitting bumper to bumper in these fume-laden tunnels that run in all directions under the streets of Paris, like the one which Princess Diana died in. I was not really liking it that much. It took us nearly three hours to get to the hotel; what a hotel, though! It was worth the effort. It was on the Place du Concorde next to the Champs-Elysées. I just cruised for a while before doing a few internet interviews and checking out the Eiffel Tower.

I was really super-tired that night, jet-lagged to the max. I tried to stay up all day, but it was the middle of summer. The following day was also the longest day of the year! That night the sun didn't set until 11.30 pm. Having just flown from the other side of the world, it was doing my head in!

WEDNESDAY 21

I FELT A LOT BETTER in the morning which was just as well, for I knew I was in for a busy day. Reid, Carl and myself played golf on the outskirts of Paris. It was bizarre, an 18-hole course in the middle of a racetrack. I was asking when race day was, thinking I could combine two of my favourite pastimes, but of course I learnt that race day wasn't when it was golf day. I could see why, obviously. What if you sliced your ball and copped a horse or a jockey in the head?

I did heaps of things that afternoon, press and media interviews, and even a television studio interview at TF1. There was a massive free music festival that day in Paris as well.

It seemed like there were musicians and bands playing everywhere you looked. Oasis played in the middle of a street about 30 minutes from where we were, but we went and saw Roger Hodgson, the ex-frontman of Supertramp. It was good. We had a private party booked and there were some journos laying in wait there, so there were more interviews to do. It was a bit of a late night.

THURSDAY 22

AFTER A BIT OF A sleep-in, I had to do a few interviews at the hotel but nothing else was on until the press launch for the Billabong Pro that night. The press conference was at an Aussie bar somewhere in Paris. It was pretty packed out; a lot of press and media were there. Billabong must have been happy. Earlier in the day we realised that I'd completed most of my interview commitments. I wasn't booked to fly out until the following day, but we changed my booking that afternoon. Accordingly, when the press conference finished at 9 pm, I raced off to the airport to catch an 11 pm flight home.

Funnily enough, when I got back on the plane it was the same flight crew as I'd flown in with. They thought I was a weirdo doing Paris in only two days. I was just happy to be on the plane heading home. It was a long flight, all the way back to Singapore, and then onwards to Brisbane.

FRIDAY 23

I WAS HIGH ALL day! About 35 000 feet high most of the time — not that I would have known. I like my sleep at the best of times, but after you've flown halfway around the world to stay at your destination for just a few days, and then get back on a plane to fly back the other way, it's only natural that you're going to be zonked by it all. I was back in business class, upstairs in the hump, and I reckon I was asleep within minutes of take-off, and it was there I stayed in zzz-land until a short time before we touched down in Singapore. While the plane refuelled, I refuelled with a beer at the bar, then got back on the plane and went back to sleep.

SATURDAY 24

AFTER NEARLY 24 HOURS in the air, we touched down early in Brisbane and I got my bags, cleared customs, and then found that there were no rental cars available. My only alternative was to jump in a limousine with all my boards and stuff. It was absolutely freezing cold. I couldn't work out how to turn the heater on in the back of the limo, and it was the first time the driver had driven it, so he didn't know either. I was spewing.

I spent the rest of the day hanging out with Bea and Rainer. I went for a quick little surf at Duranbah but the waves were tiny. Around mid-afternoon I watched the horse races on Sky, and had a few bets, but didn't do any good. As happens after a massive flight like that, I was feeling quite jet-lagged, so I went to bed early.

SUNDAY 25

I TREATED MYSELF TO a Sunday morning sleep-in. It was great. Mid-morning, I went for a surf at Duranbah. There was a kids contest on, so there we were in amongst a huge crew clearing the

water for the grommets. It was classic. Bruce Lee, Robbie Cohen and myself successfully cleared the water and had an empty line-up to play with, in between the kids getting the waves they wanted for their contest. It was good fun. After that I went home and watched rugby league all afternoon.

I watched the Newcastle Knights play the Parramatta Eels. I had another early night because I had to fly out again at 6 am. Gone again! It was off to Jeffreys Bay in South Africa for the Billabong MSF Pro.

MONDAY 26

I WAS SUPPOSED TO meet Luke at the airport, but he wasn't there when I checked in. I walked around the place and there was no sign of him. I was freaking for Louie because flights to South Africa don't leave every day of the week, and if he missed his flight he'd miss the first round of the contest. I got on the plane and still no sign. Finally, just before they closed the aircraft door, in rushed Luke. He'd checked in at ten minutes to six, for a flight leaving at 6 am. He was so lucky to make it! They're good people at Coolangatta airport.

We flew to Sydney and then went into the Qantas Club. I'd caught so many flights in the previous week that I went and tried to get an upgrade for the Sydney to Johannesburg flight, but they wouldn't do it. When I got on the plane I went up and sat in business class anyway, but it was just to Perth. When I got back on in Perth I ended up with a row of seats to myself, so I was happy. I didn't have a bad flight.

TUESDAY 27

AFTER LANDING IN JOHANNESBURG the previous evening we had to spend the night in the Jan Smuts Holiday Inn at the airport. It's a major pain in the butt every time we fly into South Africa. Our flight from Sydney invariably lands about 30 minutes before the last flight for the night takes off for Port Elizabeth, which is the nearest airport to Jeffreys Bay. Needless to say, it always takes way longer than that to clear Immigration and Customs, so we always have to spend the night in Jo'berg. It's bloody expensive too. Those airport hotels are raucous. The Holiday Inn costs about 690 Rand for the night, which is less than 200 Aussie bucks, but in relative terms it's radical. The average South African would need to spend more than a week's wages to stay there for one night.

So we caught the first plane out in the morning and touched down at Port Elizabeth an hour later, hired a car and set out for J-Bay which is a quick hour's drive south. There was Luke, Dave Rastovich and myself in the car. You run along a straight and pretty boring freeway for quite a while, then you go through some winding hilly roads, and then suddenly you start descending from the hills onto the coastal plain that leads to Jeffreys. At that point you can see Jeffreys Bay in the distance, this massive urban spread cloaked over a big, broad, jutting peninsula. As it came into view we said to Rasta, who had never been there before, 'There it is! There's Jeffreys!' He called bullshit on us. Like everyone else, he'd assumed it was a tiny little town.

Obviously it used to be a small town, but these days it is actually documented as the fastest growing town in South Africa. It seems to spread further and further west every year. Mind you, only about 10 to 15 per cent of all these brand new houses have people living in them. Most of them are just holiday houses. Some of them have incredible architecture, but many are downright ugly. Afrikaners definitely have their own sense of what is style.

Driving into J-Bay, I was having full-on flashbacks of the first time I drove into the town, back in 1984. It was obviously way, way different. It's a bummer that grommets like Rasta can't know that place and others as they used to be. But such is life, such is progress, or something like that. We pulled straight up to the point at Supertubes to check the surf and were surprised as well as stoked to find it was a nice clean 3–4'.

Straight up, we also saw our very good friends Aary and Cheron Kraak, who run Billabong/Country Feeling in South Africa. They are two of the best people you could ever meet, and they live in one of the best houses in the world, right on the point there. It's also one of the most open houses in the world: dozens of people come and go there every day, as though they live there. The Kraaks, their kids Chio, Aary Junior and Cheyenne, and their housekeepers Di and Ebby, are just the best hosts you could ever imagine. The very first overseas event I won was Cheron's Country Feeling Classic at Jeffreys in 1984. Cheron just loves the boys, and would do anything for anybody. She's my South African mum. I love her. Yeah, so Jeffreys remains a special place of special memories for me.

After all our hugs and hellos, Louie and I went for a surf. Joel Parkinson, who had been on the same plane, was already out there, as were a couple of other guys. It wasn't too bad a session, pretty damn good actually. We all had some really good waves. As tradition demanded, we went and had a nice dinner that night at the Breakers restaurant. Heaps of the crew go there every night. It's expensive, but not when you do the dollar conversion. It's usually good food too.

WEDNESDAY 28

WE FOUND THE SWELL had dropped a lot when we got up. The waves were pretty small, but we had a little surf. We needn't have bothered because it really was no good. It was breaking right on the rocks; we virtually went rock-hopping. I knocked the fins out of my board too. Bugger! I took them down to Marc Spowart's factory to get fixed and then stopped off for lunch.

After that we had a little surf on the lefts around the front of the point at Boneyard. It was OK. We probably had dinner at Breakers again that night.

THURSDAY 29

THURSDAY WAS PRETTY MUCH the same as Wednesday. Heaps of crew went to the local lion safari park, but we just hung out all day and did absolutely nothing. It was good. Yes, and we had dinner at Breakers.

FRIDAY 30

Another nothing day. We surfed a couple of times, sort of. It really was small. We just had to get wet though, because we hadn't been sleeping well, presumably because of jet-lag. When it's night in J-Bay it's daytime in Australia, so it takes a little adjustment. Don't surf, you don't get tired, and then you don't sleep.

We had a surfers' meeting that night at Greville Mitchell's rented house, which is just over from the contest tower. It was the best meeting ever, with about 40 of the top 44 present. It's a real mission to get pro surfers to an organised gathering. We can all be pretty lazy, but we're getting better. Greville is the best, and I don't think we'd be here without him. Anyway, we formed a body called the WPS — World Professional Surfers — which will be the voice for all the surfers' opinions and needs. It's a really good thing. After the meeting, just for something different, we went to Breakers again.

july 2000

July

›››› SATURDAY 1

SLOTHING AGAIN. I STARTED fantasising and figured that maybe if I got a pair of booties (they're neoprene slippers to keep your feet warm in the surf), like I had when I won J-Bay in 1984, the surf would get as good as it was that year. It was 6–8' and absolutely perfect for the final of the Country Feeling that year. Those were the days! I'll never forget it, surfing against Tom Carroll. It was just so perfect.

Anyway, I was thinking aloud to Louie and asked whether he thought it'd work. I get carried away with wishful thinking sometimes. 'Well I don't think so, but you can try,' said Luke with a bemused look on his face. So off I went to buy some booties. I never wore them though, and it never got anything like 1984. I had a good steak at Breakers that night.

SUNDAY 2

THE SWELL CAME UP to about 4–5' overnight and I think I was the first out there. Just like at home, I'd been up every morning at

5.30, hoping for waves. It's kind of tough getting up early because it's not first light until about 6.50 am there in July. The sun actually rises about 7.30. When the contest started, I watched a few heats. I watched Mick Campbell pull through his heat via a barrel on his last wave, and I watched Powelly have his first surf after having a ripped medial ligament in his knee fixed. He looked pretty good, and I was glad about that. I watched Rasta surf J-Bay for the first time, and he looked real nice, as he usually does. After that, Luke had a heat and strangely blew it by catching too many waves. He got his wave count of ten up too quickly, and left his opposition their pick.

I surfed next and it was pretty good. I got a nine-point ride, which always helps. I had a little nap after that and then got up and watched some more heats. I watched Taylor Knox and Nathan Webster, and they were both surfing well. Ross Williams ripped. I thought he might have been the best surfer of the day. In the last heat I watched Beau Emerton win, so that was good too. It was all good! We went to Breakers again that night, lovely Breakers. Maybe they should give me free meals after this book comes out. Whaddaya reckon?

MONDAY 3

After having an early surf, I settled back to watch the second-round heats. I had a day off, while the losers were redrawn to surf man on man in the quick-death second round. My travelling mate Luke Egan, being the highest-seeded surfer to lose in round one the previous day, was the first heat of the day, and he absolutely smashed young South African surfer David Weare, who was Cheron's wildcard. Cheron just loves all her grommets, but especially Davey. He's a good surfer too; he just needs more experience, like you always do when you're setting out in this game. Actually Luke must have started a trend that day, because all the wildcards got smashed.

I watched lots of heats that day. Later in the afternoon, we just kicked back in our rented apartment there at Supertubes. Beau came in with the contest draw and we worked out that I'd have Andy Irons the following day. Andy is always a tough heat. It was funny because at that point I was surfing against the guys I'd just been on the Op boat trip with. I had Tim Curran in the first round, and now I had Andy.

TUESDAY 4

I HAD AN EARLY SURF, as always, but the waves were kind of inconsistent so they moved the contest to Boneyards, which is up around the point, right in front of Cheron and Aary's house. It was alright, but there were some good waves down the point. It was a tough day because I wanted to go down the point, not surf Boneyards. Luke reckoned there wasn't enough waves and that Boneyards was the right call, and he proved he was right when he quite convincingly won his heat up there. He tactically and physically out-surfed Keith Malloy.

By late morning they were debating whether they should move the heats back to the point. Sunny Garcia was in the heat before me, against South Africa's big-wave charger, Sean Holmes. Sunny reckoned he could beat Sean at Boneyards, so he wanted it to stay put. 'You can move it when your heat comes up,' said Sunny. So Sunny surfed his heat at Boneyards and he won, even though Sean scored a 10 late in the heat. Munga and Cheron were then asking me whether I wanted it moved back to the point. I agreed that we should, presuming that they'd get the water cleared and we could go for a surf out at Supertubes and see how it was.

Andy got out there and caught a couple, and then they'd kind of cleared the water by the time I got out there. Willsy and some other crew that were there were saying, 'It's pumping! It's pumping!' With that in mind, I waited and waited, and it wasn't pumping at all. Maybe it had been; it pulses a lot like that, but it wasn't for our heat. I went over a couple of really average 2–3' waves thinking, 'Wait for a wave!' but they *were* the waves. I waited

a bit long — Luke said he was scared for me — but I ended up getting a few of those smaller ones, got a few scores, and felt like I had a good heat in the end.

Beau lost after that, which was a bummer. Then I watched what was one of the best heats of the day, a real close one between Joel Parkinson and Taj Burrow. Taj didn't go a wave at the end of the heat when he needed a 6.5. From the beach it looked like it was good enough for the score, but obviously not from the line-up, because he didn't go. Then we went to Breakers again.

WEDNESDAY 5

SHANE POWELL AND JAKE Paterson had a heat early, just about when the sun came up, it seemed. Powelly waited a bit long for his waves. Then they had the chicks' heats, and they had really good waves. We were all psyching watching on. It seemed that the waves were seriously back, but then it dropped off again when it came time for the men's competition. Luke had a super-close heat, beating Rob Machado with like a minute left. Then Peterson Rosa beat Sunny Garcia and, needless to say, Sunny wasn't too happy about that. The waves for those heats were rubbish. They were thinking about calling it off again, but then they sent the girls back out, and blow me down, it got good again. It wasn't fair!

Straight after it was the guys again. I was against Damien Hobgood, and I had the choice to have the schedule suspended, but seriously, for the sake of the event more than anything, I opted to go out, and that was probably a mistake. I was thinking that I could comfortably beat him, but when I got out there the waves were shocking. It turned to shit, the wind turned onshore and I sat there for at least 10 minutes, maybe 15, without having a wave and I was like, 'Oh shit, what have you done?'

Essentially, I blew it because I was trying to get away from Damien. He was trying to secure the inside at the start, so I didn't really hassle him. I just tried to sneak down the point and get away from him. I took off on a wave to get down really wide where the waves were breaking, knowing it wouldn't be a score, but just to get away from him. The next set was good though and he got the best of it. Then there were no sets. A bit later I got a 6.0 on a small one, but he got another and just shut me out. That's the way surfing is sometimes. It's really frustrating when you come to a classic spot and it doesn't break classically. I tried every trick in the book to make the swell come up, like buying my booties, but it didn't work.

The funniest thing about that whole episode was what Damien said after the heat. You know, I really love those Hobgood brothers. They're real good people. Damien said, 'I've got to tell you, and I've told you before, but you've been my favourite surfer ever and I so wanted to surf against you and beat you.' He really poured his heart out to me after he beat me and I'm like, 'Fuck, don't worry about it, good on you.' Then he was reminding me, 'Mate, it was your call to surf or not' and I'm like, 'Are you kidding me? How about a re-heat?' Yeah, as if!

Joel Parkinson had come up to me before my heat too, because he was in a heat after mine. Joel asked, 'What do you reckon? Do we stop or do we go?' I replied, 'Yeah there's waves, let's go.' I should have waited, but you know — shoulda, woulda, coulda; same old story. Actually, Joel did a great aerial in his heat against Shea Lopez.

We went inside then and watched the tennis. We saw Mark Philippoussis lose to Andre Agassi at Wimbledon, and then we saw my mate Pat Rafter make the semis. Guess where we went to dinner that night?

THURSDAY 6

THE SWELL DROPPED AGAIN and Munga, our touring mate, now contest director, had to can the proceedings. Munga had done well, he always gave us the choice, and that's where I blew it. I should have opted to not go out for that heat against Damien. Yep, so Munga is doing a good job.

It hit me laying in bed that morning that I'd just finished probably my worst Jeffreys campaign ever. I've been coming here for 17 years or something, and every year it seems to get a little bit worse, and this year was definitely the worst. I also wanted to change my ticket so I could get out of the place, so I was up at 5.30 trying to do that. My travel agent Deby, from Taylor Made Travel, is the best. She knew straightaway that I wanted to change my ticket, and had me confirmed on that night's flight in less than a minute. I went for a walk after that, because there was no surf.

I got my contest winnings, ate breakfast, and then we had a press conference announcing our WPS unification. Sunny, our WPS president, handled all the questions well. I think it's really good. I've always wanted the surfers to be united. After that, me, Luke and Sarge went for a drive down the coast to Oyster Bay. We nearly choked on those long dusty roads. There must have been a hole in the floor or something. Because the event's waiting period was slipping away due to the lack of swell, we were sure that the event was going to be shifted down there, so Luke wanted to have a surf.

When we got down there we found Joel Parkinson, his Dad Brian, Rasta, Dean Morrison and a few other crew about to pull out of town. They'd left Jeffreys about 90 minutes before us, but hadn't yet surfed. The tide was low-ish, and so we looked up the beach and saw a reasonable bank. It was nothing special, but we'd driven all that way so we decided we were out there, Parko and the crew as well. As we were changing, Jake Paterson and Richie Lovett rocked up as well, so down the beach we went, an instant crowd. It didn't matter though, for the beach was totally deserted, as it almost always is.

I thought the right was kind of dodgy, so while everyone surfed it, I paddled out and surfed this left. It was outside of the right, because the right was like a semi-shorebreak and the left was out the back. No one would go out there though, because Oyster Bay is a really sharky place — well, the whole of the South African coast is actually. I used to surf Oyster Bay all the time by myself though, so I went out the back by myself and surfed the left. It was kind of spooky and indeed sharky. Spending as much time in the water as I do though, I don't care about sharks. You've got more chance of being hit by a low-flying jumbo than of being eaten by a shark. The left was good. I got really barrelled on one wave actually. Everyone else was surfing the right. Oh yeah, Taj and Noodles were there too. I was telling Luke, 'Listen, if the contest is here you've got to go out to the left, don't just hit on the right, you can get two more moves on the left and then go right' and he was like, 'Yeah, yeah, yeah.'

I left that night and found that Billabong's co-founder and boss Gordon Merchant was on my flight. I had a drink with him at the airport. It had been a long time between drinks, and we hadn't spoken since our indecision on my contract after the world title. We hadn't been on speaking terms really. We met at the bar and he had a couple of Chivas Regals and I had a few beers. We talked about this and that, but nothing relevant to my contract. One thing he did say to me was, 'I'm finally going to have some money in my own pocket,' to which I replied, 'What do you mean?' I kind of knew what he meant, because ever since Billabong started he's always filtered all the money he's made through Billabong straight back into the company — apart from his $8 million house (just joking, Gordon!). I know what he meant; that is, where the money was going to come from. We all knew that the company was going to be floated.

Actually it had started — the float was on. 'I'm really excited by how much money I'm going to make out of the float,' he said, and I was like, 'Good on ya!'

FRIDAY 7

AFTER BEING ON THE flight all night, we touched down in Perth. As soon as we landed we found that there was a baggage handlers strike on. They'd walked out no longer than five minutes I reckon, or maybe 10 minutes, before we'd landed. We should have had a two-hour connection, but we waited and waited. As soon as we got past 8 pm we knew we couldn't take off, because you can't land in Sydney after midnight. I looked at the time and went, 'Oh, the plane's not going anywhere!' The baggage handlers came back on at 10 pm, apparently. We went to the casino, myself and ASP chairman Wayne 'Rabbit' Bartholomew. Gordon didn't come. He just stayed in the Qantas Club. Actually my old footy team, the Cronulla Sharks, were playing on the TV in the lounge. The Sharks won that afternoon, and we had a few beers, albeit feeling rather weird. It was morning in South Africa, which is what our bodies had adjusted to. Anyway, we finally got on a flight at midnight.

SATURDAY 8

AFTER YET ANOTHER NIGHT on a plane, well just for three or four hours, we were back into the Qantas Club in Sydney just in time

for the business rush hour. Connecting up to Brisbane, I found I'd made a big boo-boo. I'd left my passport and ticket and all that stuff on my seat in the Qantas Club. I'd gone to hire a car, but discovered I had no credit card, so I knew I'd lost my travel wallet. I was freaking! The guy from baggage services rang the Qantas Club though, and they had it, so we hired a car. We drove down to the Gold Coast, dropped Gordon off at his mansion, and then I dropped Rabbit and Shelley off at their house. We'd gone and checked Duranbah and found the waves were kind of alright. I then went up the hill to Bilambil and home to my honey.

Loving being home, I just kicked back in my armchair and watched the footy and relaxed with my wife all day. I had a long nap in the afternoon, which I shouldn't have, because I really like to stay awake every time I land in the morning. I slept most of the afternoon actually, and only caught the last half of the game I was watching. I was feeling super relaxed though, looking forward to five days at home doing nothing — well, not doing nothing, but not going in a contest. It took a sleeping tablet from Bea to get me to sleep that night, but I sure slept good.

SUNDAY 9

I HAD AN EARLY SURF at Duranbah. The waves weren't too bad, but it was kind of wintertime and high-tide, and breaking really close to the beach. There wasn't a lot of room to move, but I had a little surf and then I went and played golf.

MONDAY 10

I WENT AND PLAYED a game with my local golfing mate, Bone. We played golf all week actually. That day we played up at Palm Meadows and I won nearly $100 off him. We usually go up to $100 if we play longest and closest to the pin. If we get a birdie we get $10, or for a par we get $5. I've taken a couple of hundred off him over the years. He was like, 'Let's just play $50 a game, because you're not back enough at the moment.' And I said, 'Shit yeah! You kidding me? Fifty a game — no worries!' So we had $50, plus the longest and nearest and everything and I won like $90 off him. It was an enjoyable afternoon. Overall, it just felt good to be back up at home, and doing the routine things that you do at home waking up and surfing and playing golf.

TUESDAY 11

I WENT AND HAD AN early surf at Duranbah and then played golf again with Bone. I got too cocky and he beat me, taking $60 off me. The main thing, though, was that I was getting ready for the social club comp on Wednesday.

WEDNESDAY 12

I SLEPT IN FOR a change and found the surf was kind of small. I only surfed for about half an hour. I wasn't really interested in the surf, to tell you the truth. When I have a big long surf, it affects my golf because my shoulders are all too tight. Then I can't swing the club that well. So, I had a little surf and felt good.

After my sleep-in, by the time I came back from a surf it was time for some brunch. I had a nice egg and cheese toasted sandwich from the top shop at Bilambil.

Back at home I actually even practised putting in my lounge room, and then Bone came up and got me. It was time to play golf up behind my house on the Terranora course. I could play golf until the cows come home, I love it, so how lucky am I that our home backs on to a golf course?

◎ ◎ ◉ ◎ ◉ ◎ ◎

THURSDAY 13

I WENT AND PLAYED golf again, and didn't really even want to know about surfing. It was a full-on golf week.

◎ ◎ ◉ ◎ ◉ ◎ ◎

FRIDAY 14

WITH A CONTEST ON MY doorstep, I had to get wet, so I surfed in the morning at Duranbah. It was getting real small by that stage. The waves weren't very good, and it turned out to be an expensive surf because I buggered my back. I was going from a right to a left, you know, the right was really thinning out and the left was coming towards me. I kind of just did an extended turn from a bottom turn and went to hit the left coming towards me. I over-extended, and my back just went *doodge.* I felt it immediately and I was like, 'Fuck. Don't do it to me!'

It was the same problem that I've had since I was a young grommet. When I was about 13 years old, I slipped my disc in the Australian amateur titles when I turned pro at Avalon. I think Todd Ingham won that year. Anyway, I was in the semis and I just somehow did this turn. It's a really young age to fuck your back, but I fucked it. I had to go straight to the chiropractor before my next heat and he tried to click it in, but my back has never properly clicked in since. I think it's because I've got such a small solid back, with a low centre of gravity. They tried to whack it in but it didn't do anything and that was the start of my back problems. Then I did it again at Duranbah, the same recurring thing which I've had for all these years, and I had to hop on a plane the next day. I was dreading it.

SATURDAY 15 > TUESDAY 18

I DIDN'T SLEEP TOO well, I was so worried about getting my flight. Fortunately I got upgraded to business class, thanks to one of the air stewards who used to live at Cronulla, where I was born and raised. I still wasn't that comfortable though. It was an irritable flight the whole way. But I got to California and my back felt a bit better. I don't know why, but somehow at 35 000 feet above sea level your back kind of swells up.

I thought it was better, but my first surf I felt it and I was worried. The contest was coming down and I was trying to surf in front of my Huntington Beach hotel, the Waterfront Hilton, and I was in pain. For three days it got worse and worse and I got more and more concerned.

I was spewing about my accommodation too. I'd stayed there for the previous four years and always had a good room overlooking the famous pier and the contest. Last year when I stayed there with Bea, we had a really nice room. To someone who lives in Australia it's not really the best view, but it's maybe one of the better views you can get in California.

This time, though, I'd checked in and they'd put me in a room overlooking Huntington Beach, but looking over the back side of Huntington. I was not happy. What's worse, they were charging me US$290 per night, or something like that. I rang Bea and told her how I was spewing and she said to say something, so I did, and they changed me to a room overlooking Huntington at $20 cheaper. It just goes to show if you don't say something you get nothing. The room was twice the size as well. I was like, 'Are you guys kidding me?'

I've got a bit of history at Huntington, too, after winning the event several times. It's a special place for me; I've got some really good friends there, like my mate Danny who's been at Huntington forever. I've got new friends there as well, like Johnny, although I don't actually know where Johnny is these days. He used to work at the Waterfront Hilton as a waiter/room service guy. He worked at the place for years, but this year when I got back he wasn't there anymore. I found out they'd sacked him. I think maybe it was my fault, because he used to spend way too much time in my room having beers and stuff, maybe when he was supposed to be working. Sorry, Johnny.

WEDNESDAY 19

For some reason my back felt OK before my first-round heat. It was pretty bad though after I'd lost my heat! I had Shea Lopez and a young South African whippersnapper named Simon Nicholson. I didn't have too much of a bad heat, but Simon was hassling me, hassling me bad! I turned to him during the heat and I was like, 'Fuck! Listen mate, we don't hassle in three-man heats!' He said, 'Ooh, I'm sorry, I'm just a rookie!' I thought, 'You sure fucking are!' Anyway, I had one eight-point ride in that heat but not a lot else. I didn't feel too good. In the end I'd needed just a five-pointer, but it didn't come.

I had been real confused before the heat about what board to ride. I ending up picking and surfing a Wade Tokoro. Sunny had been surfing Tokoros really good there, and Ross Williams had as well. That shouldn't have influenced my decision, but since I'm saying it did, I guess it did. I got an 8.0, so that was something but that was about it. Not good.

I had to do a promo late that afternoon, but we had a surf first. I went down to the pier with Kalani Robb. You can't often surf on the south side of the pier there, because it's usually blackballed. That's when they put up these signs with a big black circle painted on them and it means that no surfing is allowed in that area. We walked down there, about to paddle out on the north side of the pier, and this lifeguard pulls up in one of those *Baywatch* cars and says, 'Do you guys want to surf the right side of the pier?' We were like, 'Are you kidding me?' and he says, 'Yeah, it's OK, just go down and grab a singlet. You can surf out there.' We were stoked. We ran down and grabbed singlets. There was no one out there, not a soul. We paddled out there and I had a good surf.

I had a new board from an American guy who shapes Dahlbergs over in the States, the guy who does Mayhem Surfboards. The board felt fine and Luke came out for the arvo's surf, saw me surfing and said it looked good. When I showed him the board on the beach later though he's looked it over and said, 'There's way too much bottom curve for you.' I was thinking like, 'Shit! What does bottom curve mean?' He kind of tried to psych me out of riding the board. I'm hopeless with the technicalities of surfboards. I just surf them, and if they work, they work. If they don't, I get another one.

Later that night I ended up going with Luke all the way down to Dana Point, where he was staying. It's a bit of a hike, but heaps of crew don't like staying in Huntington itself; so many, including Luke, stay down at Dana or Laguna or San Clemente. Fair enough. Anyway, Luke and I went to a Japanese restaurant down there, which was pretty decent. We'd wanted to go to the Chart House, but it was packed. I told Luke when he dropped me off that if he needed a bed because he had an early heat whatever morning, I had a spare bed and he was welcome to stay.

THURSDAY 20

I WAS CONFUSED PRETTY much from the moment I got out of bed. I had a crucial heat to surf, three surfboards, and I didn't know which one to surf. I had my Dahlberg, a Tokoro, and the Mayhem. I'm like looking at these three boards, and I'm in one of the early heats because I lost as top seed, and I'm like, 'Shit!' To make matters worse, I had actually slept in because I went down to dinner with Luke down the coast. I woke up in a panic. My first waking thought was, 'Fuck, what board do I ride?'

As the name would suggest, the Waterfront Hilton is right on the beach, so I just ran down the front with the Dahlberg and the Mayhem. Neither one felt that good, so I towelled both of them and surfed the Tokoro. I probably made the wrong choice. I surfed my heat against a former top 44 surfer from Brazil named Joca Junior. He's a formula man, particularly quick and flashy in smaller surf, which it was. I started off well. I had a seven and felt

good. I was talking to myself going, 'Yeah, solid, you'll be alright,' but then he started getting a couple of good waves and I started trying too hard. I couldn't seem to get any more good scores and he went into the lead.

At the end I needed a five-pointer, and right then I got the wave to do it. I did two turns that I thought were shitty. I didn't think I'd get the score I needed, so I went for a big last turn and fell off. *Drat!* They gave me a 5.1 and I needed a 5.2. I was cursing myself silently, screaming, 'What did you do that for?!' I came in and everyone was asking me the same question and I'm like, 'Shit, I didn't think I had the score.' I hadn't needed to go big on that last one after all. I'd blown it. To make matters worse, I'd hurt my back after attempting the manoeuvre.

Actually, that's a lie. I didn't hurt my back on the fall at all. After that wave I still had two minutes left, and I only needed a real small score, 5.0. I got this little right and tried way too hard on it and I ruined my back and came in. I didn't let on to anyone, but I was just hobbling up the beach in agony. Oh, my goodness. It was really, really bad.

So that was kind of depressing. I went all the way over there and I got a 33rd. I didn't like it one little bit. I went back to the Hilton, got a smoothie and just lay in bed. I was so upset. I had to do a promo for Globe that afternoon at 2.30 and another one later on for Billabong, but the way I felt I just wanted to fly home that night — really badly.

I rang Bea to ask her to take up the mission to change my flight. Normally I've been able to get out of California any day, any time, but Bea rang me back and said, 'Mark, you can't get out tonight' and I'm like 'You're kidding me?' and she confirmed the bad news, telling me the flight was totally full. I was devastated. So I had to go and do the Billabong promo. Later I met up with Danny and we had a few drinks.

FRIDAY 21

NEEDLESS TO SAY, I just hung in the room all day waiting until it was time to head for the airport. I didn't want to know about the contest. I didn't go out; didn't go to watch the contest or anything, just hung in the room and then got on the flight that night. Danny took me to the plane. We were really late getting to LAX actually. I thought we were going to miss it, but I got on and all was fine. I then spent the next 16 hours, or whatever it was, winging back home to the centre of the universe.

SUNDAY 23

WHEN YOU FLY BACK to Australia east to west, and cross the international dateline, you lose a day. I'll never forget flying back from Sandy Beach in Hawaii one year after the old Gotcha Pro there. This was back when I was a grommet on tour. I took off from Honolulu on 15 June, and arrived 17 June. So? Well my birthday is 16 June, so technically I never had a birthday that year. I was born on 16 June 1966, so that should make me 34, but since I missed that birthday, I'm saying it makes me 33!

So 33-year-old me got home, and once again my back felt better after the flight. I checked the waves and they were pretty small, but my old surfing partner was too busy to go surfing anyway. My stepson Rainer was moving out of home. I didn't want him to move, but he's got Chrissy, and Bea thought it was the right thing for them to move out because Rainer was abusing the principle of being home and getting free rent and free money and free everything. Beatrice decided to deny those privileges, so Rainer moved out. I didn't really want that because I love going surfing with Rainer every morning when he's up to it. Yeah, so I wasn't real happy about it but hey, kids grow up, don't they? Rainer was out of there and I was tripping on it. Me and Bea were at home all alone. But having that big beautiful house all to ourselves felt pretty strange.

Rainer got himself a nice little flat down at Coolangatta, close to the main street, close to where he's got his new job. He's working on a book with a mate of Rabbit's named Steve Row, who got a grant from the government to do a book on the development of boardriders' clubs on the Gold Coast since the 1960s. Rainer and the other crew working on the project are going around interviewing people about the clubs, even older clubs like Windensea. Rainer seems to like it. His girlfriend had a job at the Calypso bar, where Rainer was spending too much time. Rainer would go and wait for her to finish work and have a few beers. But you know, he's growing up. He's just turned 18 and he's doing good.

MONDAY 24 JULY › FRIDAY 11 AUGUST

THREE WEEKS CRUISING AT HOME! How good is it! Three weeks at home. It's so rare! Most mornings I went for an early surf, but not always. Some mornings I'd just watch the television and watch the golf. The British Open was on while I was home. I watched Tiger Woods do a remarkable job of it.

While Sarge was interviewing me for this he asked whether I ever looked at other athletes, like Tiger Woods, who are the best in their field, and compare myself to them in terms of publicity and dollars. The answer is nope, not really. Tiger makes golf look really easy, like they all kind of do. I guess we make surfing look easy too.

I love golf and my snowboarding, but surfing is just so much better than anything else. I reckon we've got it so much better, even though we don't make the money that golfers and tennis players do. We make up for it in how much enjoyment we get out of just practising. I mean those guys just go out there and hit balls, thousands of balls, for hours, but we can go and surf and get barrelled and just get totally stoked, or get that special wave that comes to you, or go through a really good period of weeks where you're surfing perfect 6–8' waves every day. Or, you get that good 10-foot swell and get a big adrenalin rush. I mean there's just so many things that can make you high from surfing — not to mention winning contests.

Yeah, so I flashed on snowboarding just before. When I flew home from California the snow report said it was the best season they'd had for five years. My gut instinct was to head down to the Thredbo. I really wanted to go, but I didn't just have a sore back but a sore wrist as well. I had a wrestle around with Luke and Hoyo in Fiji, when we were drunk on the last night, and I hurt my wrist. I still wanted to go snowboarding, though.

I asked Luke but he didn't want to go. Rainer couldn't go because of his new job. Bea said, 'Don't tell Rainer you're going' because she thought it'd unsettle him in his new job. At one point I was going to go it alone, but going solo is not as much fun as it is with mates. To tease me even more, I got a snowboard sent to me from one of the snowboard companies, Force. That was nice of them.

When I went surfing, it was usually at Duranbah which was ok, usually about 2–3'. I surfed there most mornings, but there was also a really good bank happening at Rainbow Bay the first week I was home. I can especially remember surfing there one morning and it was so perfect. It was only 1–2', but they were just the best waves you could hope for. Nick Wood was out there, pulling in, getting barrelled, but I couldn't quite fit in there on my back hand. It was that small. I felt like a kid again because when I was a grommet, with my Kurnell mate Richard Maurer we used to surf Kurnell Point, especially when it was small. It used to be really hollow and we used to call out to each other 'laydowns!' We wouldn't stand up, we'd just lie down in the barrel. That was the only way you could fit.

So there I was at Rainbow Bay, thinking of Richard Maurer, just lying down in these barrels. You could slide your board, so I waited to fit in with the wave, slowing down. It was like Kirra. I was sitting in barrels lying down and even pumping it and stuff. I was getting barrelled for 10 seconds, maybe longer. It was so much fun. I just stayed out there for hours doing that. The local grommets were out there too, having fun themselves, and no doubt amused just watching me lying down. Sometimes I'd stand up, but my back was a little sore too. I stood up a few times and did a few turns, but not much.

After that surf, pretty much after *every* surf I have in the vicinity of Coolangatta, I made my usual morning pilgrimage to the

Healthy Bee for a carrot and beetroot juice, and a ginger and watercress juice for Bea. Carol, my beautiful second mother, gives me a little sweet every time I go in there. Her husband Barry is always there reading the paper. I always ask if he has any tips for the horses. We talk about the races and how we did on our previous bet.

It was funny thinking of Richard that first week while I was surfing those miniature barrels at Rainbow Bay, because he rang me the following weekend on the Saturday afternoon. It was the first preliminary final of the ARL and the Cronulla Sharks had just squeaked in there and got eighth spot. They had to deal with the Brisbane Broncos that day. It was a really good game, and at half-time the Sharks were kicking them 20–6. That excited Richard, and he rang me at half-time from Cronulla.

We were just hooting on the phone and he was going, 'They're going to win! We're going to get para' tonight!'

'Yeah, I'm having a couple too!' I agreed.

It looked like we were going to freight train them, so Richard hung up, saying he'd ring me after the game. However, in the second half the bubble burst and the Broncos just went berserk, as they do. They beat us. There was no phone call after the end of the game either. I crashed out pretty early that night finding it a bit upsetting that the Sharkies were out of the competition. One day!

Yes, you guessed it, I played plenty of golf in that three weeks as well. A couple of days after I got home I played golf with Tweed Heads barber Richard Smith, Blairy and Jay. Include me, and that's the foursome that I always play with every Wednesday. The first Saturday of every month we have a monthly medal. On the Friday before our August monthly medal I was playing with

Margo and Bone. The course was set up as hard as it could be — all the tees were up the back and all the pins were in the hardest places. I don't want to brag, but I was on fire. I had a really good score and had to be extra careful at the end.

It was my best round ever. I was just floating because I broke the nineties!

I got a score of 87. It was something I've always wanted to achieve. For the past five years of playing golf I'd never broken into the eighties, and that day I didn't move the ball once. Oops! You know, obviously you don't move the ball, but I've enjoyed playing over the years with Richard Smith (we call him 'Alleybarber', but his other nickname is 'Preferred Lie' because he always takes a preferred lie). He'll kill me if I say this, but he taught me how to do preferred lies. If your ball's laying down a bit too deep, you just lift it up a little, as though to check it's your ball. Then you say, 'Oh yeah, that's mine', and then you give it a nice fluffy lie. I'm sure everyone has done it at one time or another. I didn't do it once that day. I was stoked.

I really wanted to go up to Surfers and go mad and stuff that night, celebrate, but I didn't. I contained myself and just went down to Seagulls, had a few beers, and told all the patrons about my score. I was quite proud of it.

The next day we played in the monthly medal and, sure enough, I couldn't do it twice in a row. I just couldn't do it. I think I shot something like 97. We finished early that day to watch Easts play Penrith.

Sometime in that three weeks Luke and I went to South Straddy. We habitually ring each other on our mobiles at 6 am each day to work out where the best waves are. On one of those mornings, Luke rang and I reported that Duranbah wasn't that good. Besides that, I was actually sick of Duranbah. 'Let's go to Straddy,' said Luke. 'Yeah, why not. Where will I meet you?' I asked. Luke answered, 'Oh shit! I just spilt my coffee all over me.' You get that when you drive a five-speed manual Falcon juggling a cup of coffee and a mobile phone. As it turned out, Luke was already halfway there with his jet ski in tow. I gave chase. You'd think that at 6.15 in the morning there'd be no traffic but I hit a backlog of traffic going through Surfers Paradise — every traffic light was banked back at least ten cars deep. That's nothing compared to any city in the world, but on the Goldy in winter that's a traffic jam!

Meanwhile, Luke's heading for South Straddy at about 180 km/h. When I eventually arrived and parked my car, Luke was like, 'Where have you been?'

'Peak hour. Sorry mate,' I replied.

Louie doesn't like waiting. He expects punctuality. Louie rules. So I jumped in my wettie and we fanged over the Seaway to Straddie. It's great fun on those jet skis. We zoomed into the break to check out where the best bank was and then he dropped me off before going off to anchor the jet ski off the break.

There was a few crew over there that morning. Sam Watts was there, as well as most of the boys from DHD, Darren Handley's surfboard company. They had their jet ski there as well. The waves were pretty shitty, but I was having a ball on my Mayhem board. I was really loving it. I just wanted to catch any wave that came at me. I was stoked that day, but no one else seemed to think they were having a good surf. I was going, 'Are you guys kidding me?' I was getting little airs, really smooth turns; I could even look back sometimes and see myself snap off the lip — it looked real good.

While I was doing that, all the guys got bored, and decided they'd turn it into Waterworld. They decided to get their skis, have one guy on the front, one guy on the back, and do these things called 'step-offs'. They were chasing every little swell that moved, and really bumping the line-up, so I moved off down the beach and got away from them. Louie is really good at those step-off things. They go flying across the peak; Louie just simply side-saddles the jet ski and places his board down on the peak when they're doing about 60 km/h, and does a massive take-off and turn, straight into the wave. It's a radical sight. Another time I was watching him do it at Tweed Bar. It's radical. I surfed for another hour or so while they played with all that, and then we bailed.

We actually went to Straddy two days in a row. The second time something bad happened; nothing to do with me, but one of those territorial surf things. I remember Margo and Luke telling me that they often get into hassles with body board riders over at Straddy. It has never happened to me, though. At Duranbah, where I usually surf, the boogie board riders are pretty cool. We know a few of them, as does Rainer; there's one called 'Dave da Booger'. Most of the boogers there are cool. If you're going for a wave they don't hassle. It's cool. It's well controlled.

Anyway, this second day at Straddy, we'd got up early. It was a bit bigger and cleaner, so we jetted over there and went through the usual procedure. Louie had dropped me off before anchoring the jet ski and then paddling back into the lineup, asking, 'How is it?'

'Pretty good fun barrels,' I replied.

A good peak came and I took it, took a late drop, and the wave curled around. Luke was on the same wave going right, just down the beach. I pulled into a really nice tube, and Luke must have been watching me in it. I came flying out of it; just squeaked out before it connected with the right. It was a really fun wave.

I surfed for about an hour or so, and then Luke asked if I wanted to go. I said 'Yeah' and he paddled off to get the ski. While he was doing that, this peak comes up. It was a good peak and so I paddled over for it. There was a young boogie boarder in the take-off region, young but big. He started acting like he was going to drop in on me and I started yelling, 'Hey! Hoi!' I took the wave from the right and backdoored it through the left, and he broke it down on me. He still looked like he was going to drop in on me, but then he pulled back and, as he did, he yelled 'Hoi! Hoi!' back to me. I thought, 'That doesn't happen every day.' Usually they just pull back and don't say anything. It was my wave, and I was paddling for it first. He broke the tube down on me, but I made it through anyway.

As I was paddling back out, I was thinking, 'Why did that guy say that?' So I paddled up to him and said, 'What did you say, mate?' He replied, 'I said "Hoi"!' He was really aggressive. I asked why, and he snapped back, 'Because I wanted to.' I thought 'Shit' and then he just started calling me out. When he said, 'You're a poofter!' I should have just smacked him. I told Luke about it later, and he wanted to go back and do him, but I reasoned that he wasn't worth the effort. This guy went on, 'I don't reckon you're number one, you don't charge Tahiti. We charge Tahiti at 12–15'; you guys are only out there at 6–8'. Maybe someone should point out to them that we stand up, and they take the easy way out and lay down. I said, 'You know what grommet, you've got a lot to learn!' Then he started mimicking me. Everything I said, he'd shadow back to me. He was a cent short of a dollar.

He kept doing it, trying to get me psyched to hit him. He obviously wanted a fight.

I should have just said, 'You're nothing!' — which he was. You know, that famous old Andrew Johns saying, 'You're nothing!' At the time, I didn't have any comeback because I just couldn't believe this goose. Over all the years I was surfing huge Hawaii he was still in nappies. I don't know who he was, or if he ever charged Hawaii, but who gives a damn anyway. Anyway, so I did the wisest thing and paddled away from the loser. I went back knowing, 'Well, not everyone loves ya!'

One really heavy task while I was home was to attend a funeral. It was very sad and moving. My golfing mate Jay's wife Annie had died. She'd been sick with a rare cancer for years. A lot of people from Bilambil were there, and a lot of kids. She was a real special woman and they have two special children, Corinne and Damien. The funeral was down at Tweed and the wake was at the Twin Towns Services Club. Jay went to Vietnam so he was entitled to support from the club.

Death is such a heavy thing. Everyone is going to die sooner or later, and it's kind of weird you know. I mean it's one of those things that you've just got to learn to accept. It's hard even thinking about it. I love life so much and I've got such a good one. I'm really grateful. But death is really tough to think about.

Towards the end of that same period, my mum rang me to tell me that she was on the Gold Coast. She lives back in Cronulla but she was up for a week and was staying with my sister Fleur, who lives at Bilinga. I dropped in there on my way to golf the same day she rang, but they weren't there. I kept ringing her mobile, but it never answered. It would have been great to see them both before I went away, but it seemed it wasn't to be.

Mum ended up ringing me on my mobile the next morning and apologised for missing me. They'd forgotten the time and gone shopping. Unfortunately, I didn't have time to see her that day because I was heading off to France the following day and just had heaps and heaps of things to do. She told me she loved me, as she always does, and wished me luck in the European leg. I love her too — heaps!

My mum is really solid at the moment, just powering and totally loving life. She's retired and plays heaps of bridge. She loves bridge. She's just really happy, you can tell. I wouldn't be here without Mum. She used to drive me down the coast and to any contest I ever wanted to go in. We did so many miles in her old silver Toyota Celica. She even drove me to Western Australia three times for contests — nah, only joking, but she would have if I'd asked her. She used to drive me to South Coast Pipe when the swell looked right — when I should have been at school — and would sit there in the carpark after a three-hour drive and read a book all day while I surfed the waves. She let me have time off school whenever I wanted to surf. She always said, 'You're going to be a champion, Mark!' She never doubted it, and gave me nothing but total loving and support. She's a big reason why I was so successful, that's for sure.

I didn't get much of a chance to train over that three weeks, because my back was too sore, but I did have a couple of little surfs at my favourite backbeach, Fingal. The last couple of days before I left it was breaking down there, and I ended up running into my Aboriginal mate Scottie Rotumah. He told me he had been painting traditional Aboriginal style and he showed me his board which had an all-time mural painted on the bottom of it. I said, 'Wow that's all-time!' It was really awesome-looking art. He told me that he wanted to paint one of my boards, and I readily surrendered the one under my arm, a Dahlberg, of course, but one made in California by Rod's man over there Rob Bayalis. Scottie was doing his art and selling it on the Internet, so he was stoked that I was keen. He said he'd give the board back to me the following weekend.

That last week at home, I also had to go and see my osteopath Geoffrey Hale and get some work done on my back. He's good, but I still had that niggling thing. The day before I flew out to France I hurt it again just sleeping the wrong way. I woke up one morning and I said to myself, 'Far out, it's back to square one', just like it had been in California. I was really worried about it.

august 2000

August

›››› SATURDAY 12

I WAS HAPPY to see Rainer down at Duranbah for the second annual Sean Fanning/Joel Green Memorial Contest. Sean and Joel were two popular and talented Duranbah surfers who were tragically killed in a car accident a couple of years back. Both were only teenagers, and there's nothing sadder than when people are taken away in the prime of life. Sean was Mick Fanning's older brother. Their deaths ripped the Coolangatta end of the coast in two. The outpouring of grief was just unprecedented.

Their memorial contest is a big event, patronised by everyone on the south end of the coast. Lots of kids surf in it. I really wanted to go in the contest, but my back was really sore. Out of respect for Sean and Joel, I ended up going in it anyway. I surfed in the team section and they started me with Darrell, Joel Green's dad, who I haven't really met before, and it was good. He's a top bloke. There was a really good and respectful vibe happening down at the contest and you could see he was stoked on it.

In my heat, I remember I sat for ages waiting for the right wave. It was just closing at Duranbah — every single wave. Darrell rides a longboard, so it was pretty tough for him, but he got some good waves. We were up against one kid who got a good little barrel, and another grommet who got one as well. He had to like double-whammy his wave and go in, so I was left sitting out there. Not a decent wave came through for almost 20 minutes and I was just sitting there thinking, 'Oh, oh.' I was high just on being there, though, being involved in such a special thing, being out there with Darrell, meeting everyone else — good thoughts and then, as always happens when you think good thoughts, a beautiful little left came to me with 10 seconds to go. I got barrelled on it, but that's about all I could do because of my back. Still, we ended up getting through.

Margo came down and surfed with Darrell in the next round. I was with Rainer. He had been out of the water for a few weeks with a sprained ankle. I got him a wetsuit and board out of the storeroom and we tried to go for a surf, but my back was still really sore. He couldn't surf, so he gave his spot up to John Harrington, a really good little surfer from the Gold Coast. He rips.

I couldn't play golf that afternoon because I was leaving the next day. Instead, I went home and watched the racing channel. I backed a couple of winners. I backed a winner called Addition. 'Le addition' in French is 'the bill'. When you're at a restaurant and you're full and ready to leave, you say, 'Le addition, s'il vous plait.' Don't ask me what that's got to do with anything, but it just struck me. I was going to France the next day and thought, 'Oh yeah, I'll go for this.' Even though it was 32–1, I put $10 each way on it on my phone tab. It kicked out from the start and just got like ten lengths ahead in no time. It was obviously a roughie, though, so I thought it was bound to be swallowed up. The rest of the field caught him, but then he kicked again and won! I was so happy. Whoops, there I go talking about gambling again. As Sarge has been turning our taped sessions for this project into written words, we've been progressively reading the finished text. One comment my wife Bea made was that I talked about gambling too much. Gambling is just a game to me, and it may seem that I do a bit too much of it, but honestly, it's not as rad as it seems. I never lose any massive amounts, and even though I bet big sometimes it is only a minute portion of my income in the big picture. Isn't money made to enjoy? Bea manages our finances and I just get a little bit every week to play with. It's just a game — entertainment! I don't encourage it. Like all things, it's good to indulge but not excessively.

SUNDAY 13

I WENT BACK DOWN to the contest to collect my board from Scotty Rotumah. He gave it to me and it looked great. I was really stoked. We met in a perfect spot right in the stairs at Duranbah. It felt really special. He's a real special guy, Scotty, a hot natural-footer and a good-looking guy. I dig his dreadlocks. He won the last indigenous contest too. Just to meet him and get the board felt like some sort of tribal offering; I felt really honoured to have that turtle painted on my surfboard.

After packing the board, we basically hit the road. Bea and I hired a one-way drop-off rental car because we were flying out of Brisbane. Driving up from Coolangatta, I felt like pulling over, my back was that sore. It was really sore to sit down, and especially to drive. I was wondering how I was going to fly; I was really dreading it. We got to Brisbane and as we were checking in some of the airline staff, who I knew from surfing, upgraded both me and Bea, giving us two business class seats all the way to Singapore. I was stoked. From Singapore to London they said we'd have to try our luck. We tried but we were put back in economy — bad economy. Flying from Singapore to London was a bit of a horror flight. It was a new flight crew, and one of the stewards knew me, so I thought we might still be a chance, but he said the plane was full and I believed him. The steward looking after my section in economy was being a real dick. You know, it's just a grovel back there in economy. Since I won the world title I get so many people coming up to me, going, 'What are you doing sitting back here?' I like laugh, 'You know.'

MONDAY 14

WE GOT TO LONDON and that's where I had to say goodbye to Bea. While I headed for France, Bea was going to hang in England for a week with Jackie, Russell Winter's girlfriend. After London, they were off to Cornwall. So we landed in Heathrow and went through Immigration and then we had to say goodbye. We're used to it, I guess. I sat next to Michael Lowe on the plane from London to Bordeaux. You know I always sleep on flights, but Lowey and I didn't this time. We talked the whole way. I really dig Lowey. Like my wife says, he's one of my better friends and I agree with that. He's really genuine. He's such a good guy. He's a great surfer too. He charges. He was talking about how he's been having a shocker and I'm like, 'Yeah, the last couple of contests haven't been real good for me either.'

When we landed we collected our boards and stuff and picked up our leased cars. Every year, when we get to France, we get brand new cars. I mean brand new, with like five kilometres on the clock. It's unreal, kind of an added bonus to our annual European occupation. We lease them from Renault France. Renaults are French cars obviously, probably the most popular brand there, like Commodores in Australia. They're unreal. Between all of us WQS and WCT surfers we probably lease about 20 or 30 of them every year. Anyway, Lowey was going to follow me to Lacanau. I've 'only' driven there about 15 times but, like always, I wasn't sure I remembered the way. He was trying to explain the way to me — I'm just not good on directions — but somehow we got there. We'd heard before we arrived that the waves had been real flat for a month, so we were really glad to arrive and see waves. They were like 4–5', and the trials were going down.

It was late afternoon, really glary, and my back was really sore, but I wanted to go and get wet. I waxed up a longer board, a 6'5", and paddled out. The waves were really flat and I couldn't do much at all with my back being as it was. I got a couple of rights, but I was thinking, 'Shit, you're in trouble.' My back felt really weak. But I did stay out for about two or three hours. I don't know why. I just had to paddle around and get wet after all that flying.

TUESDAY 15

A LOT OF THE crew don't like going to Lacanau. It's a super well-organised event, and that intolerant call from the boys is no reflection on the crew from the local surf club who run it, but the town is just so incredibly packed out during contest week that it can drive you batty. Lacanau, though, is really special to me. It was where I first won an 'A'-grade ASP event, the Tutti Frutti Pro, back in 1984. It was an apt name, because the tour really was 'tutti frutti'.

I really like the town, and I know some of its citizens well. We have a mate there called Jean-Michel Gue — we call him 'Johnny Mick' — who takes really good care of us. He was there in 1984, and he's still there. He's been to Oz, and everywhere else we go. He's solidly one of the boys. It was super-sad to think that it might be the last time I'd ever travel to Lacanau. For the first time in some 20 years, the event is not on next year's ASP WCT schedule. Hopefully they can put on a WQS or something next year, to keep the tradition rolling.

When we got up that morning, we found the surf had dropped much more than we thought it would. I didn't mind though, for I was really worried about my back. I got up early and went down to the contest to look for the chiropractor but there was no one there. I just watched some heats, but all the while I was preoccupied worrying about my back. Soon enough I had to go for my heat against Luke Hitchings and I could barely surf. I could take off and do a couple of turns, but I was in bad shape and certainly didn't feel good. I was way too stiff. It's different every time I get a sore back, but this time I was even having trouble standing up. Just going from the prone position to standing up, swinging my legs under my feet and standing up on the board was painful, and a real worry. It was really hurting. Once I got totally up onto my board I could kind of turn, but that's mainly because I've got such big ankles and feet. I can turn just with that part of my body without using my back, but that's only through years of experience. I was in no shape for anything. Right at the end of the heat I could barely stand up. I knew I shouldn't have been out there.

Obviously I can't say it was the first time in my life because I've retired before, but let's say I was seriously thinking that maybe I just shouldn't have been there. My back was that bad. A bad back is not like a broken leg. It's not like something that can be fixed by a prescription or time. It was really starting to shit me but all I could do was just grin and bear it. At least I had a good excuse for not winning the heat — not that many people were aware of it. I just watched my friend's heats after that. I watched Powelly's heat and he surfed really well, but he was unlucky. It seems like he's always unlucky, but I reckon that's about to change.

Late in the day I got my back worked on and it felt a bit better. I was given some good stretching exercises too. I was staying with Powelly and his girlfriend Michelle. We had dinner at a restaurant and had an early night, a rare thing 10 years ago. We used to always go bananas on our first night in town.

WEDNESDAY 16

I WAS IN THE second or third heat of the day, but again I couldn't go for an early surf because my back was too sore. I thought that I shouldn't free surf but save it for my heats. The surf was nice, really clean little Lacanau. It was about two foot, maybe three foot, and running nicely across the bank — not too bad for my back. I didn't really have to do much. I was against this cool French guy, Eric Ribiere. He was nice and talkative in the water, mentioning to me that summer in France was hard for him because he's young and horny. That made me chuckle. 'Oh, you poor thing,' I laughed, but he was right. It's just beautiful women galore in France in summer. It had only been three days, but straightaway I thought how much I was missing my honey just across the English Channel. I was also thinking to myself, 'Shit, you're a bit lucky, because the kid surfs good but he's only cruising.' As it happened, I got all the good waves in the heat and cruised through it easily. So that was OK. I was stoked to win that heat. I had sort of started to doubt my tactical stability and inner drive because it seems I have been losing my early-round heats lately. I had lost kind of early at J-Bay, and then got knocked out in the second round of Huntington, and that had really hurt. So I felt good after that heat; I hadn't aggravated my back injury.

After getting my back worked on again, I then went back to the apartment that I was sharing with Powelly and Michelle, and sat and chilled for a while. Before long, a lot of friends came over, among them Johnny Mick, Beau Emerton and Mick Campbell. We sat on the balcony talking and watching heats. We've hired the same apartment for years. It's such a good room because we look right over the event and the main street, where everyone walks up and down along the beachfront, is right beneath us. Some days we'd throw eggs and other days we'd just watch the parade. It was a really entertaining spot to hang out. We had a great time that day.

Powelly surfed later in the day against Greg Emslie, and he ripped. He just full-on surfed so good. We were all hooting from up on the balcony. His form reminded me of the time years ago when he comboed Kelly Slater in the same event. We were sitting on the same balcony too.

THURSDAY 17

I THINK I DREW about heat four or five and, once again, I couldn't have a free surf. It seemed like my back wasn't hurting as much, but then when I got out there and took off on my first wave, I found it wasn't good at all. The waves were about 3–5'. Usually bigger waves help, but this day the waves were so flat and full that you really had to do some big long turns and bounces to get through sections. I think I just overexerted my back. At one stage, I paddled so hard for a wave that I knew it was going to be a good one. I stood up a bit quick though, and my back started really hurting. I got in a couple of turns but I only got a 5.4. If my back had been better I'm sure I would have got a 6.0 or a 7.0 on it. My opponent, Pat O' Connell, then got a 7.25 and I needed a big score to catch him, which never came. After losing, another 17th, I was pretty upset and dejected. I felt like leaving town, but I hung in there and went and got some more work done on my back before watching Powelly's heat against Victor Ribas.

Shane surfed really good and was really unlucky. He should have won the heat on three different waves. Even though he was ripping, he still needed a 5.0 at the end, and he got it with a score of 5.5. Victor got the wave behind him, though. He really dug a big rail and blew the first turn which, as the judges will tell you, is just so important in competition surfing. He just grovelled along inside for the rest of the wave, like he often does, but still got a 6.5. It was just ridiculous. He got two inflated scores like that during the heat. Later

we watched the heat on video and all saw how unlucky Shane had been. It was unjust. But Shane's not one to rush down to the judges' tower with the video. He had a good laugh, like Shane always does, and joked, 'Yeah, I'll run down and show them.' He's such a good loser. He's one of the best losers I've ever met and it just goes to show how good a person he is. He can take anything.

Heaps of us went out that night and had a great rampaging time. We all got really pissed. It was a bit like how we used to go crazy there in Lacanau back in the 1980s. We got really drunk and it was fun. There was about eight or ten of us, and we just forgot about everything, including my back, which didn't hurt at all.

FRIDAY 18

AS USUALLY HAPPENS WITH a fairly serious hangover, it was a slow and tedious day. I managed to wake up, got some more work done on my back, and then watched heats all day from the balcony. Late in the arvo, we had dinner and a few more beers, and then I just cruised with the boys. It was mellow.

SATURDAY 19

THE SURF WAS DROPPING quick, and the contest was already up to the quarter-final stage. They should have finished the contest right there and then, but unbelievably they only had the quarters. The contest directors were obviously trying to stretch the event out, which was totally without consideration for the surfers and the surf conditions. It was lame. I couldn't believe it. I had nothing to do with it, but I felt like running down to the contest organisers and telling them off. Instead, I just sat up in my little room looking over the contest saying to myself, 'They're tripping'. The surf was already so ordinary that I was virtually sleeping between heats. Every time the hooter would sound, I'd get a jolt and watch a bit of whatever heat was on

SUNDAY 20

AS EXPECTED, THE SURF dropped to nothing, proving that the contest organisers had seriously blown it. It was pitiful, barely one foot. Jake Paterson was against Rob Machado in one semi, Shea Lopez and Armando Daltro in the other. I mean it was just *so* pathetic! On the Saturday they could have had a pretty good finish, but they weren't logical. I really like Rob Machado, and the way he surfs, but it was one foot and he was surfing a board that was like three inches thick. It was like what we used to ride in the 1980s. I was thinking to myself, 'Are they going back to that?' I mean, he was easily the better surfer on the day, but I just kept questioning why they hadn't finished the event the previous day in good waves, which would have facilitated us seeing the moves that we want to see. Anyway, that was that. I watched the final and Rob won. It was a well-deserved win, given the conditions. I looked down on the podium as they made the presentation, and recalled when I had been up there the year before. At Lacanau they always pour buckets of confetti down on the winner's podium as they announce the winner. Sure enough, the confetti came flying down on Rob and Armando. It brought back good memories. Later Beau and I had a quiet dinner and packed up our stuff in preparation for leaving Lacanau the following morning.

MONDAY 21

I GOT UP ABOUT 9 am, which is early in France, and packed the car. I'm not real good at maps or finding my way on the roads, so I rang Sarge, who was already in Hossegor, and got a refresher course in how to get from Lacanau to the freeway. As it turned out, I found my way easily. All I could think of driving down there was my back. It's about a two-hour drive and my back was really, really sore. I got to Hossegor and checked into my hotel, the Mercedes, which is right on the river there. It felt really nice to be back in Hossegor. It feels like home. I went to try and have a surf, which probably wasn't very smart, but I just wanted to get in the water. The waves were small and I did a little turn and my back went out severely. Then I was freaking, full on freaking!

Russell Winter came over later in the day. Bea and Michelle were still in England, and Russell didn't have anywhere to stay that night so I invited him in. We went and had dinner together with Beau and Sarge at an Italian joint in the main street and then stopped for some ice creams on the way home. They really get into their sweets and desserts in France, and their ice cream is especially good.

TUESDAY 22

I WOKE UP STOKED because Bea was flying in that day, and I was looking forward to getting some sympathy for my sore back. With my back problems, it had seemed a very long week in Lacanau. It had seemed a major accomplishment just to get through the week, especially without Bea. When you've got problems it's always extra tough when you're without your partner, so it was extra good to have my honey back. Late morning, Russell and I drove down to Biarritz airport, which is just half an hour down the freeway from Hossegor. We were both really happy to finally see our partners again. It was good. We went and ate McDonalds on the way back up to Hossegor, which is a bit of a treat in France. There are only a few McDonalds outlets in French regional areas. They have a few in places like Bordeaux and Paris, but overall they're hard to find. After McDonalds we all drove back to Hossegor and, since it was a really hot sunny day and the ocean was flat, hung by the pool for most of the afternoon.

That night we went out to dinner at a high-class restaurant on the lake at Hossegor. We had the famous Moules Marinières, which is a bit of a French specialty that we always get. I really liked it, although Bea got sick later and had diarrhoea all night. Maybe it was something she ate on the plane, or the McDonalds, because I didn't get sick. I love the way the French eat. To them, eating is a celebration of their lifestyle, a tradition, and they really take their time at it. Being half-Italian, I also love spending a lot of time with my meal and savouring different courses. I don't like eating in a hurry, wham bam down and out of there. It must be said, though, that France is really hit-and-miss on the restaurant scene. You can get some really excellent meals, and then you can go to another supposedly reputable restaurant and get a real dud. You can go for days having dud meals. They don't eat as healthily as we do in Australia, either. Health food shops are ultra-rare.

WEDNESDAY 23

IT WAS BACK TO the contest routine for the start of the Rip Curl Pro, just up the beach from Hossegor, immediately south of Estagnot. In need of work on my back, I went down to the impressive contest superstructure on the beach and sought out the contest masseur, an Aussie guy called Justin. Apparently he'd just finished three years of studying massage and, as people often do after intensive study, he was now travelling through Europe. As it turned out, he knew my doctor sister Fleur, having worked with her at the Billabong Pro on the Gold Coast. Justin was really good. We had a classic workout, and he gave me some good stretches and loosened me up a lot. I felt I had more mobility than what I'd had the entire previous week in Lacanau.

Feeling much better, I went out and surfed my heat. I surfed a board I'd been wanting to surf since I'd arrived in France. I actually had quite a good heat. Considering my back, I thought I surfed really well. I got a lot of positive comments from people, saying how good I surfed and how good the board looked and I was like, 'Wow'. I was stoked and inspired. People don't usually come up to me and say, 'I really like the way you surfed.' There was only one problem, though. One of my opponents, Andy Irons, got a freak barrel and scored a 10. I don't know if it was a 10 because I didn't actually see it, but it's hard to get a 10 on a four-foot beach break. To that point I'd been leading the heat, so I was like, 'Shit, that puts me behind the eight ball.' I ended up nearly winning the heat, but I didn't and I was kind of pissed off. It would have helped if had won because I would have gone straight into the third round and got a day's rest for my back. I'd got some good waves and done some big turns and my back had suffered for it. I just went home and told Bea about it, and she was like, 'Don't worry, at least you surfed good.' She was right.

THURSDAY 24

I GOT UP AND went straight down to the contest site to see Justin and get some more work done on my back. I felt extra-tired. He couldn't move me around like he had the previous day. I had to reassure him,

'No, it's not you, it's me. I'm really tired.' I told him not to push it because it felt too tight, so I just had a light workout.

That morning there were waves around three foot, but then, as happens in Europe, the tide got too high and the waves filled right up. It eventually stopped breaking at high tide, and they put the schedule on hold right before my heat. I was drawn against Toby Martin and we were the first heat, back on a few hours later when the tide went out. The tide hadn't gone out enough though. I appealed to the contest director to stop and hold the resumption off for another half an hour, but they said they were running out of time. So I then pleaded with Perry Hatchett, the head judge, 'At least give us 30 minutes,' but he just shook his head and said he couldn't. I can't see what harm it would have done. I swear, the waves were breaking about five foot from the beach, and it was really bad. I didn't want to go out, but I had to.

I wasn't happy, and didn't hassle enough for the first wave. Sure enough, in the end that was the decider. I more or less put myself in the position to say to Perry 'Listen, you should have given me five more minutes' because right at the end of the heat a set came through, and I would have probably got the score I needed. It just wasn't fair. They're trying to ensure pro surfing is better, more appealing and in performed in better waves, so their decision to go ahead in really marginal conditions was just unbelievable. It just didn't need to be done because they ended up having swell at the end of the event. I was really bummed with Perry, Rip Curl and contest director Charlie. I walked up the beach thinking, 'Far out, that 's just so not happening.' I would hate them to do it to someone like Kelly Slater, or Sunny Garcia, who's leading the ratings so far this year. I hadn't had a good showing for a few events, but I was the current world champion and there they were sticking me out in total shit. I was wondering, 'What's the use?' I was really pissed off. I went home and told Bea and she was like, 'Far out. You're having a shocker.' I went, 'I am', but she was encouraging me, going, 'It'll be alright, you're just going through a bad run.' She made me feel better, like she always does. Instead of drowning my sorrows, I took it easy, had a quiet dinner and went to bed.

FRIDAY 25

AFTER THE PREVIOUS DAY'S debacle, I woke up tempted to go into self-destruct mode, but I didn't. By the time I sat up in bed I was feeling good. I'd lost the contest, and my back was bad too, but I felt alright. I was saying to myself, 'Come on, get back on track.' I sat around at first, really bored, but the waves looked fun so I went for a surf.

I went up to Bourdaines with Mick Campbell and his fiancée, Cheree. Mick did an aerial in front of me, and then I did one in front of him. It was really cool. It seems everyone on the tour is doing aerials at the moment. It's really good. Later in the day I played golf with Russell Winter and it turned out to be a good move. I was just so sick of not playing golf and not free-surfing because of my back. I was also sick of babying it, so after I lost my heat I thought, 'I'm finished babying it. I'm going to go free-surfing and I'm going to play golf.' The surf with Mick Campbell hurt a little and I couldn't surf real good, but I was still determined to go and play golf. With the swing it seemed like it was stretching my back into place and I was kicking myself saying sarcastically, 'I could have been playing golf every day and my back would be straight.' I had a good game. I shot a 48 over nine holes with five clubs. I crushed Russell, even though he played well too. I think he shot a 53. I walked off the course one happy man that day. Later we went out and had dinner and a couple of drinks. Bea, Jackie and even Russ kicked on and went out, but I went back to the Mercedes.

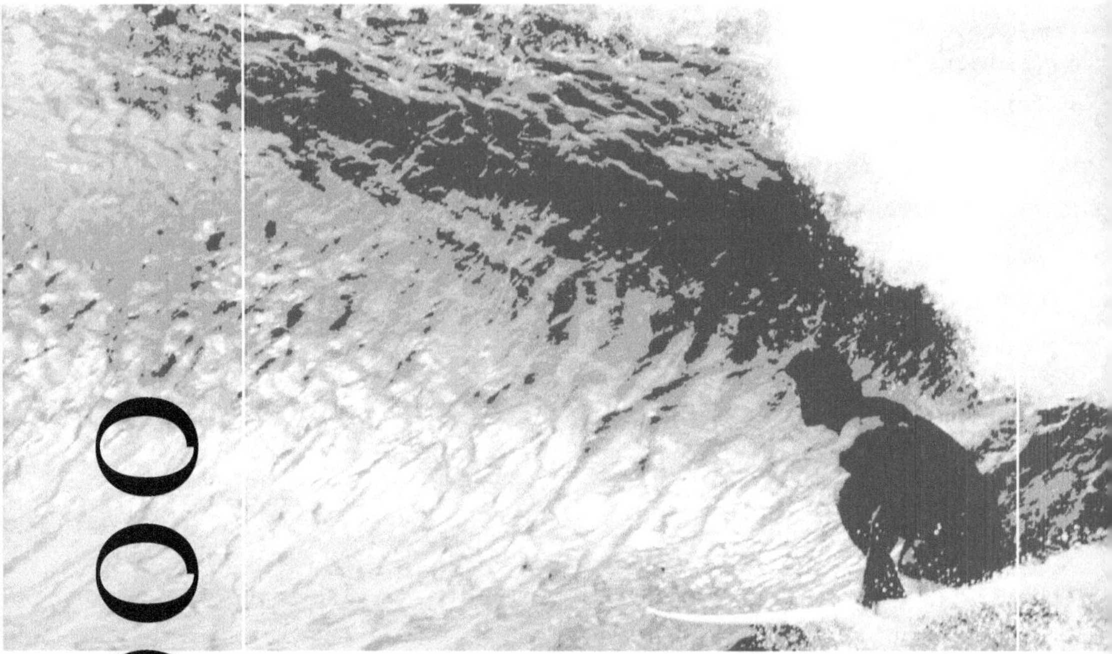

SATURDAY 26

The swell was really dying and the waves were getting really small. I knew one thing — I didn't want to go anywhere near the contest that day. I did hear, though, that both Luke and Sunny had got through their heats. I'd watched Luke the day before against Conan Hayes, and he got really lucky. He was winning the heat after making a great comeback and then right at the end Conan needed only a 5.2. He did two nice turns but then bogged his rail, so Luke got through. It gave him a second wind in the event. Instead, I went back to the golf course and had another round with Russell. I play golf with Russell a lot, mostly on the Goldy. He's got a really good full swing on him. I reckon he could get really good at it, and that's what I keep telling him, but sometimes he has a shocker and he wants to throw it in. I just tell him, 'That's golf.' He beat me, though. I shot something like 60 over nine holes. Russell got 50, and it was his best score ever.

SUNDAY 27

ONCE AGAIN, I DIDN'T watch the contest because it was real small. Louis got through to the quarters, though. I saw him that afternoon and said, 'Good on you, great.' We all had a drink that afternoon, smack bang in the centre of Hossegor at the Cafe de Paris. It's the best spot for drinking in the world, and for watching the world go by in all different shapes and sizes — mostly good shapes! We christened our drinking session the Matt Hoy Remembrance Day. Hoyo was everyone's mate and we're missing him so much already. The Cafe de Paris was Hoyo's favourite drinking hole. It seemed like he'd go there every afternoon for a beer or three. They've got these things we call 'giraffes', which Hoyo made a Hossegor institution. A giraffe is a perspex cylinder of beer with a tap at the bottom, all on a stand that you plonk on your table. It's a great idea because four or five people get a couple of glasses of beer out of each giraffe. It's like having a mini-keg on your table. You just sit there with one in front of you and pour beers for your mates and yourself, and then order another one. The beer doesn't stop flowing. They should have them in Oz. They could call them 'Hoyos'. He'd love that. We had a great session. Everyone came, basically every Aussie in town, plus a few other crew. It was a really good fun afternoon.

I was really tempted to go out afterwards because Russell and a whole bunch of crew, really amped after that little session in the afternoon, were going out, and Bea and Jackie too, but I stayed behind. I had a couple of beers with Luke though, then got a pizza and went to bed. I just wanted to go down the contest in the morning and give Luke some support because he was the only Aussie left in the quarter-finals. Apparently it was a massive night down at the Rockfood. The girls got home at three in the morning.

MONDAY 28

I THINK I MIGHT have been one of the few Australian ASP surfers who woke up that morning feeling good, though I actually missed Luke's quarter-final. I thought it started at 8 am and I got up way before that. There were a few small waves and it was quite clean, so I ran down for a surf at Bourdaines. Later, when I got down to the contest, Luke had already won his heat. They were surfing the back-up bank, north of the big superstructure, the same one I'd lost to Toby on.

I was walking down the beach and from a distance I could see that Ross Williams was surfing, and I thought, 'Geez, that's after Luke's heat.' So I went down there and Luke was sitting there, all smiles. It was obvious how he'd gone. 'I won! I'm in the semis.' I apologised for not making it and he said, 'Don't worry about it, it's good.' That stunned me a little. 'Shit. Do you want me to go?' I said. I'm quite superstitious, you see, but Luke just laughed. So I sat down, and watched the last quarter-final. Luke was in the following semi. For a change, I didn't get hassled by all the French people on the beach. They're real autograph-hunters, probably the most fanatical in the world. When I'm walking around the streets here, or in the carpark, 95 per cent of the time I don't escape walking past a group of people without being recognised. They look at me and then, about ten steps later, or less than ten, they're yelling, 'Hey stop, photo, autograph.' It was quiet down there that morning, though. It was only about 10 am, which is way before most of the French get out of bed and open their shutters.

The organisers were racing to get the quarters, semis and the final finished before high tide. Because the swell was so small it was pretty much a given that the incoming tide would fill in the swell and it would stop breaking. Luke got changed, gave me his seat and then walked down the beach for his heat. I sat there, drinking his water, cheering him on. He ended up beating Shea Lopez. Shea was surfing good, though, especially considering how weak the waves were. Conditions were a lot like Florida, where Shea is originally from, but big Luke surfed great, picking the better waves and pretty much waxing him.

Then our mate Greville Mitchell rocked up and asked me if I wanted to go in the MSF expression session. Grev pays out US$15 000 at some of our contests, about four or five I think, and puts on three rounds of expression sessions. It's just for the boys to earn some more cash, as well as to entertain the crowds. The French, in particular, really love expression sessions. They're a cultural people, and they seem to appreciate self-expression, be it on canvas or in the surf. I'd go in the espression session for nix anyway; in fact, all of the boys would do anything for Greville. Even so, when I looked around and it seemed like there were hardly any of the boys around, I thought 'Yeah, I'll get money!' But when I returned from getting my board from the car, Corey Lopez and all the others had turned up. Bummer! Corey almost always wins Greville's expression sessions with those incredible airs he seems to be able to pull off at will. I did a couple of small aerials, but nothing to beat Corey. All of us came in as Luke and C. J. Hobgood prepared to paddle out for the final. I wished Luke all the best of luck and then sat down.

Luke had asked me earlier about whether I thought the lefts or rights were better. Because of the incoming tide, I considered that the lefts were shaping up well, but I reasoned that the high scorers would be on the rights. The banks change radically with the rapidly moving tides in France. As it turned out, Luke paddled straight into a left. 'Bad move,' I thought to myself, but he surfed it really good, doing some nice turns, really solid all the way to the beach, and got a 6.75 which was a good start. C. J. got a little right and didn't score as high, so he then moved over to the left. Luke swapped him and moved over to the right and got some big scores. He got an 8.5 and an 8.0. I can't remember all of them but he was a long way in front, so C. J. needed a 9.0, which would normally be a massive task. Somehow, though, C. J. just seemed to squeak his way back in there. He got a 7.75 and then another 7.75 and then only needed a seven-point something ride. He took off on this little wave that Luke kind of let him go on. It didn't look like the big scorer, but he surfed it complete and people turned around to me going, 'What do you think?' The wave height definitely wasn't worth the score. He didn't catch one rail, his last turn was ridiculously good and he surfed the wave perfect. I said, 'I think he's going to get the score.' Which he did.

We would have had a big night again at the Cafe de Paris for Louis, but it wasn't to be. I left the beach almost straightaway. Obviously I would have stayed if he had won. Our French mate Johnny Mick arrived just as I was walking up the dunes. He'd driven down the freeway like a maniac from Lacanau when he heard that Luke was in the quarters. I had to tell him that he'd lost. Johnny Mick, always positive, just laughed and said, 'Oh it doesn't matter, he got second, that's still good. It's a real good result.' He was right, of course.

I went home for a nap and then Louis came and grabbed me in the afternoon. We went down to the Cafe de Paris for some beers, his shout, and it was good. Johnny Mick was there of course, and Sarge and Beau Emerton dropped in for a few too. Little did we know, it would be a big night for Beau. After the beers, we drove down to Capbreton, which is south across the Hossegor River, and went to this really good Thai restaurant. We weren't intending to go out afterwards, but then we had a nice bottle of wine. Pretty soon, Luke and Johnny Mick were really keen on doing something. 'We'll go out and have just a little look,' I suggested. We had a little look and there were a lot of people down at the Rockfood, and so we kind of kicked on. I had one of my first nights out in quite a while. I didn't get back to our hotel room until 3 am, and Bea wasn't happy. I said, 'Shit, you can't talk!' She'd had a few late ones herself earlier in the week. It was all good. Hossegor is all good.

TUESDAY 29

A DAY OFF FROM contests. Yahoo! That probably sounds like I'm being a spoilt brat, but sometimes, especially in the European leg, we have back-to-back events, week after week, with usually just a single day's break in between. It can be really gruelling — logistically, physically and mentally. Anyway, I woke up in the morning and was a little bit hungover. I didn't get up until about ten o'clock, and for me that's really late. I went to check the surf and it had picked up, not a lot, but it was about three foot, maybe four foot. The wind was offshore too. It looked real nice. I grabbed my board, and went up to my favourite bank at Bourdaines. It was perfect. It looked like a little St Leu or something. In case you don't know, St Leu is a famous wave in the Reunion Islands, which are off Madagascar, near Mauritius. I first went there in the mid 1980s where we made part of the movie *Pump*. It's an awesome wave that bends around the reef and is super-hollow and shallow on the inside.

The surf was so perfect but, to be honest, I still felt a bit under the influence. I still paddled out though, but I could certainly feel the effects of the night before. We'd had quite a few drinks. I didn't really care — I was just 'soul' surfing, free-surfing … having fun. I was pulling into little barrels with some beautiful little sections in them. I didn't even bother turning; I was just soul arching it. The looser I got the more I would start doing different roundhouse cutbacks and stuff. I felt really good and loose. The back wasn't hurting and I was stoked. I was really stoked. I surfed out there for two hours with Mick Campbell and we were loving it. After coming in, I had a nice nap while Bea was sunbaking down at the beach. It was a beautiful hot summer's day, about 36°C — really good.

After my nap I just kicked back until Sarge came around to interview some more for this book. He had some heavy news. Apparently, early that morning, our young mate Beau Emerton had arrived back at his Anglet motel and discovered that he had lost his room key, which also opened the foyer door. There was no night desk or call button, so he decided to scale the outside wall up to his balcony. He got up to the balcony, but then lost his grip and fell backwards, about five metres. He landed on a large flat plastic flowerpot. The loosely packed earth inside it luckily broke his fall. Even so, he still hurt his back, and had to get five stitches to the side of his head where it struck the corner of the adjacent marble steps. He was so lucky. Our masseur mate, Mayumi, who has successfully helped out heaps of pro surfers over the years with his traditional Japanese medicine and massage, took Beau to be x-rayed, as well as organised a brain scan. Beau had 'just' a hairline fracture to a butterfly bone off his vertebrae, plus the stitches. His brain scan came out all-clear. If he wasn't so fit and such a headstrong mongrel, and if that pot wasn't there, or he had fallen a few inches to the right, fully onto the steps, the situation might have been as heavy as it gets. The incident kind of shocked everyone. Beau is a classic — really treasured by everyone on the tour. He's like the Aussie crew's eternal little brother and I was freaking as Sarge told me the details of his accident. Thank God he was more or less OK.

WEDNESDAY 30

FOR SOME REASON, I found it quite hard to wake up and get up. The French summer is just so long, and the nights are so short. The Rip Curl event at Hossegor is always a big week socially, and last week was no exception to the rule. I mean, I've been in France for three weeks now, and it seems like forever. Just to go out at night a little bit really sets you back. Even if you don't go out, it's hard to wake up early because you're not getting to sleep until about 10.30 or 11 pm. It doesn't really get dark until that time so you might not even get to sleep until midnight. It just drains you.

So I had to wake up early to drive about 40 minutes down south to Anglet for the first day of the Billabong Pro Anglet/Mundaka (that's what they call it). I was scheduled in an early heat, the third one, so I had to go early and it was tough to wake up. I was knackered but I really liked the drive. It's always nice cruising down the freeway. I drove down to Biarritz, then back north through the beachfront city to Anglet. After all that, I found the contest wasn't on. It was high tide, and the waves were really small.

As a PR thing for Billabong, we ended up having a little surf with some little local grommets and even pre-school kids. The pre-school kids were fantastic. They were only about two-foot high and some of them had three-foot long surfboards. They were just so into surfing. A couple of them were so amped. It reminded me of when I was a grommet. Some of their parents insisted on having their picture taken with Taj, or Lowey, or myself, any of the Billabong crew that were there, but I could tell they didn't want to be there for a photo — they just wanted to get out there. As soon as the all-clear was given, they just bolted for the surf so quick they were tripping over their leg ropes. I was thinking, 'That's so classic.' Even though the 'waves' were pathetic, it felt really good to surf back at Anglet, where I won the contest the previous year, and there I was taking all these really young toddlers out surfing. I think more contests should do that sort of thing. After that I drove back to Hossegor and played golf later in the afternoon.

THURSDAY 31

It was back down to Biarritz to find that the waves were still really average and, to make matters worse, the wind was onshore as well. It was a bit of an ugly scene. We waited around for a while to see what it looked like it was going to do on the dropping tide, but then the organisers eventually postponed the men's comp and placed the women's on standby. In the end they had the first round of the women's event. Reportedly it got to about three foot on low tide, but was really messy. The surf looked even worse, and it was smaller back at Hossegor, so I went and played golf. The days are so long that it's hard to gauge the time, especially in the afternoon. French afternoons just go forever. Just before sunset, ASP Chairman Rabbit Bartholomew came around to our room to fill me in on some new things that are happening with the ASP. It's all looking good. Since we formed the WPS in Jeffreys Bay, and all the boys started acting together on issues and stuff, it seems like we're really moving ahead. Naturally, a lot of credit for that has to go to our mate Grev, who is giving us good advice and guidance.

september 2000

September

›››› **FRIDAY** 1

I WOKE UP EARLY, FEELING probably the brightest I've felt since being in France. I knew the surf was flat because, since we'd started at Anglet, the tide had been high every morning around 8 am. It was 9 am on this day. At high tide though, the swell has to be over six foot to be even thinking about breaking. So I drove down to Anglet, even though I knew that the contest wouldn't be on. But as I was drawn in the third heat, I had to be there, just in case.

Sure enough, the contest wasn't on. I had to do a little media job for Crystal, the event secretary and staff coordinator. She's super-organised, and she did a great job that week. She wanted me to give her a quote about my deceased Hawaiian brother Ronnie Burns which was going to be used to promote and publicise a junior contest that Billabong were staging in Hawaii the following weekend. Ronnie was killed in a motocross accident some years back. His death shattered me because we were like brothers. We sort of grew up together, because I used to spend extended periods on the North Shore in the 1980s. I loved him. He was a beautiful guy, and an incredible surfer, particularly at Pipeline.

After that I ripped back up to Hossegor because I had to get Bea to the doctor's for an appointment. There was nothing wrong with her or anything, but she was booked to go to India a few weeks on, and so she had to get a hepatitis injection. She was flying out the following day with Jackie for a few days break on the Mediterranean at St Tropez. That was cool with me, because I've brought her to Europe five times now and, like the rest of us, all she's really seen is surfing contest sites. She was off to do some long-overdue touristing! After I dropped Bea at the doctor's, I went around to Louie's place to see if he wanted to come out for a surf. He said it was shitty, but I went out for a surf anyway. It was one foot and it got really grovelly, which meant I had to do a lot of physical work and, surprisingly, my back was fine. It felt good. I was happy and decided to get the thoughts that I'd been having about retiring, way out of my head. Yes, that is what I had been thinking.

Since California I had been having a real bummer of a time, admittedly mainly because of my back, but I wasn't handling the frustration of that and the bad run of results I had been experiencing. I had started getting downright pissed off with it all, and was seriously considering throwing the towel in after the completion of the Billabong Pro Anglet/Mundaka. Yep, I was that disillusioned. Bea was the only person who knew what I was thinking, but then she told Sarge, who just blew up and said, 'No way!' He was right. I would probably have come to the same conclusion, but maybe I had to be coaxed into thinking positively.

Even though the waves had been crappy, I drove back from my surf thinking, 'I'm stoked being over here. I really like Hossegor,

and I'm really looking forward to this event. I'm going to do good!' Beyond that I was thinking that following Anglet/Mundaka I was going to drive to Portugal for the Figueira Pro, and then straight after that I'd be on a plane to America for the Billabong Pro at Trestles, which I was really looking forward to. 'Fuck! What have I been thinking? Everything is great!' I found myself saying out aloud. By the time I got back to the motel, I felt really cruisy and good.

Back at the Mercedes I took a little nap and Bea made me a really nice salad baguette. French baguettes are probably the best bread in the world. They go off in a day though, rock hard. Seriously, you can use them for baseball bats the day after they're made. After lunch I played golf with Russ and had a good game.

I used Carwyn Williams's clubs, some new Taylor Made sticks that I hadn't tried before. They were nice. On the way back, I filled up my car in anticipation of driving down to Mundaka the following day, because the call was that the swell was going to rise overnight. Then I checked the surf to see if it was coming up, but it wasn't coming up. Sarge then came around for dinner and to do a bit more recording for this book. Do you realise how many hours this whole mission has taken? You'd better be enjoying it! Dinner was actually the most brilliant I'd had since arriving in France. Bea cooked it and everything — the vegies, the macaroni, the steak — was so perfectly cooked. Sarge and I were both just drooling and raving. Bea just goes off in the kitchen.

SATURDAY 2

WE HAD TO WAKE UP real early, way before dawn, to get Bea and Jackie to Biarritz for their early flight to St Tropez. While Bea did a few last-minute things, I shuttled my boards down to the car and then we set off, some Steely Dan blasting on the stereo. I was holding my breath much of the way because Jackie had a bit of a raucous cough going in the back, and I was stressing about catching whatever she had. I got them to the airport on time, gave Bea a big kiss goodbye, and jumped back in the car to head down to the beach. I was really excited about seeing how big the surf was going to be, to see if we really were going to go to Mundaka. I couldn't remember being that excited since I'd arrived in Europe. I'd even had a shave the night before, and shampooed my hair and stuff — everything I hadn't done since arriving. I was like, 'This is great. It'll be good.' Anyway, I got there right on 7.30 and went up and saw the contest director, Marc Sarran. The wind was howling onshore, and it was cold too. The tide was so high that it wasn't even breaking. There was definitely swell under there, though. It looked like it might be only 3–4', though maybe 5–6'. You just couldn't tell because the tide was that high. 'Oh, we can't go to Mundaka. It's not big enough,' declared Marc. It was supposed to get bigger through the day, and it looked like it might too. I felt like saying 'Come on, let's go' but he wasn't about to budge. Once a Frenchman makes up his mind, that's that. He declared we'd have a full round there at Anglet, which was probably a bad choice, because it was pretty big, too big for Anglet, about six foot, but breaking miles out. I surfed my heat just on the change of the tide. With the tide it was progressively breaking further and further out to sea, and really hard to judge where to sit. I felt like I wanted to break down walls out there, but I couldn't find any walls to break. It was a really frustrating heat for me. I finally got a barrel about 30 seconds after the heat had finished, but obviously it was too late to be scored. It was frustrating.

When I came in they were talking about having round two that same afternoon, coming back at 6 pm and surfing till dark, which would have been about 9.30 pm. I thought that was a bit much, but it obviously wasn't my call. Someone said to me, 'You should go down to Mundaka, it's four foot.' I wasn't very happy and snapped back, 'Well, if I'd won my heat I would!' Then the contest director said, 'Well, you could go down there and have a surf for an hour and come back for your heat!' It's a good two hours to Mundaka. He was tripping. I responded, saying, 'Are you kidding me?' I'd already been down to Biarritz and back to Anglet, and now he wanted me to go to Mundaka and then back again for my heat. What did he think I was? A superhero? I went back to Hossegor for a nap instead. I wanted to go back and watch Luke's heat, but it was raining and I thought, 'No, do the right thing, you might surf again. Just rest and relax.' So I did that and put some time into myself and had a rest and went back down to Anglet. By the time I got back down there the waves looked better and I was looking forward to surfing again after all. Then the contest director told me that 10 minutes after I'd left, they'd called off the second round. Spewing! I'd driven back down for nothing. I wasn't stoked. I watched Powelly's heat while I was there. He ripped and got the highest score of the contest, a 9.4 on a right where he just

exploded three gouging manoeuvres on a five-foot onshore wave. It was really nice work. Then I talked to Preso and found out an alternative route back to Hossegor after learning that there'd been an accident on the freeway and that traffic was backed up for miles. I took the old route, the N10 through Labenne.

When I got back to Hossegor I went for a surf straightaway. The waves were nice. It had the size of Anglet, about six foot, and I surfed my favourite bank at Bourdaines. The rip was running superhard across the bank and you had to get out after each wave and then run down the beach to jump back in the rip to get back to the take-off zone. Beau Emerton had just got out of bed the previous day after recovering from his accident. He couldn't yet surf properly with his crook back, but he came down to watch from the beach. It was a beautiful late afternoon, all golden as the sun headed for the horizon. I got a really nice wave, a really good shaped one with lots of power. I got in some big roundhouse cutbacks and a snap and I tried to carve through a 360, but fell. As I got back on my board, I looked in and Beau had his arms out clapping me. I followed it up with a similar wave. Then I proceeded to run back up the beach and got swept through the bank twice without getting any waves, because the rip was so strong. As I ran past Beau he yelled out, 'You're going back out again?'

'Yeah, I got ripped off that time. Didn't get a wave,' I yelled back.

'Don't worry, you're still winning!'

Luke Hitchings, Jake Paterson and Richie Lovett were out there too, so I guess that with those two good waves I'd had Beau figured I was 'winning' the session. Once a competitor, always a competitor I guess. I was stoked that Beau said that though, because it really gave me confidence in the board I was riding. I'd still been struggling with it; it's really 'squirty' , the Mayhem one, and I'd been almost too scared to ride it. I knew in my heart though that it was a good board. 'Geez, that board looks good,' said Beau after the session. I was stoked, and decided right then and there that I'd ride that board in the contest the following day. Beau and I went to dinner that night with Luke, Johnny Mick and his Lacanau mate, Michel Boyer. Luke was a classic. He had to do something else on the way to the restaurant so he rang Johnny Mick on his mobile at the restaurant, ordered over the phone and then walked in and sat down just as the meal was being served. Just call him 'High Tech Luke'. We might have had a beer or two after that at the Rockfood too. I packed a lot into the day!

SUNDAY 3

I WAS INTENDING TO sleep in because the last three days had been really slow. High tide in the morning, no waves — hard to get motivated. There was swell, but no waves. I called Sarge on his mobile at the contest about 9.15 am and he said, 'Yeah, it won't start until 10.30, but with four women's heats, then the mens.' So I went back to sleep for an hour. I woke up at about 11.15 or so, rang Sarge again, and found that the tide had delayed things longer than anticipated and that they had only just started with the women. So I just cruised around, wasted some time and arrived with perfect timing because there were about ten minutes left in the last women's heat. Sunny Garcia was walking down the beach with local French kid Fabrice Gelez, who he was about to surf against in the first heat of the men's second round. It was an easy heat for Sunny, because Fabrice is just learning. European surfing is developing slowly, but it's producing more and more quality. They've got some good grommets on the way through too. After a bit of a hard time in the wave-selection department, Fabrice managed to get a 5.0 towards the end of the heat.

I then watched Luke's heat against Portugal's best surfer, Tiago Pires. Tiago surfed well but Luke surfed too solid for him. The heats these days are getting really important for Luke, especially in the early rounds, as he is coming second in the ratings behind Sunny. It's all getting interesting. Sunny will get through and then, instead of bailing the contest, will stay and watch Luke. Luke's campaign is still on the tracks but if he loses early and Sunny goes on and gets a good result, it could be devastating for the title race. So it's getting really tight now.

I was stoked when Luke came in. I went and borrowed some wax from him and then went back to the car to get some Barley Green. I hadn't eaten that day; I don't know why. The best food I can eat for surfing, because it doesn't fill you up, is Barley Green. It gives you all the stuff you need to have good energy. So I took some and felt nice and relaxed. I then went down the beach and caught a wave. I got a little right, but it didn't feel that good. Straightaway I was saying to myself, 'Oh, I hope I've got it today!' Then this little left came, and I was thinking about how the Bayalis board that I was riding was going, the one with the Aboriginal turtle design painted on it. Yeah, so this wave came, a little left, and I just teed off on it, just did three moves. It was just like, 'Wow! Wow!' It felt so good. I was just stoked, saying to myself, 'Oh yes!'

My heat, which was coming up, was against Toby Martin. I did an unusual thing and paddled out a few minutes early onto the bank to the north of the contest arena and caught a wave to warm

up. It was a little left, and it just gave me the right energy and space all the way down the line. I got three good moves down and flicked out smiling big time. Sarge told me later how his Dutch apprentice Johan had watched me surf that wave before the heat and then turned around to him and said, 'I wonder how Toby feels now?' I felt that too. I looked in after I got off that wave and saw Toby walking down the beach towards the water, and said to myself, 'Yeah, good. Now he knows how he has to surf.' So it was good. From there, I just paddled over to the contest bank feeling really confident. I felt a lot more confident than I've felt in a long time, probably all year. I was like, 'Yeah, I feel good.' Then a nice little right came to me, I got it, went good on it, got a 7.75, the highest score I've had in France, and I was even more confident. Unfortunately, halfway through the heat, the wind went onshore and it went a bit weird, but the main thing was I had a solid hold on the heat and, in the end, Toby needed an 8.5 out there. It was tough, so I kind of cruised around with him, but he didn't get the wave or the score. It was really good to have a win, like passing the big hump in the mountain that had previously seemed only remotely possible. You've just got to hang on in those situations. I must say it was especially satisfying to beat Toby after he had beaten me the previous week in Hossegor. Essentially, though, it was just great to have a win.

I then hung out and watched some more heats with Johnny Mick and the waves actually got a lot better. The wind dropped off and I watched some good barrels go down. I was sitting there as the tide went out, watching the waves clean up around the four-foot mark, with some five-foot sections as well. It looking just like the France we came to know and love in the 1980s when it seemed we always scored beautiful and clean sizeable swells. I said to Johnny Mick, 'Now this is France!' He just nodded and smiled, as smugly as only he can. I could see 'A-frame' peaks up and down the beach. Every wave was just coiling, barrels spitting. We watched a few heats and had a laugh with Mick Lowe, Toby Martin and Greg Emslie. We were all laughing about a few things, but nothing in particular. It just seemed like there was a good vibe in the air. Johnny Mick was just asking me questions and they were really funny, and I was just answering them back with my own twisted sense of humour. By then it was about 4 pm, and I hadn't eaten anything all day. We went back to Hossegor to my favourite little place on the lake that serves poulet (chicken) panini. I had some poulet panini and chips, the Gallic version of my old staple — chicken and chips. A little bit of indulgence doesn't hurt from time to time.

MONDAY 4

YET ANOTHER STANDBY day, so I went to my favourite little bank at Bourdaines. The surf was quite small, so I only had a short surf. A little later, Russell Winter came around to our hotel. He was blueing with his girlfriend Jackie at the time and was a bit stressed, so I suggested we go play a round of golf to get his mind off it.

We went up to the beautiful Seignosse course and then we went to the Cafe de Paris and had a few beers with some of the crew. There was Beau, Pato, Greville and Lisa Mitchell, their daughter Suzie, her friend Rob, Sarge, his apprentice Johan, and Richie Lovett and his soon-to-be (that very night, in fact) fiancée, Amanda. We found out later that Richie had taken Amanda to the cafe, engagement ring in his pocket and all, to ask her to marry him, but then when he saw all of us there he put off popping the question. He did the deed a few hours later by the pool at the Mercedes.

After a few beers I went and ordered some takeaway pizza from Benny's, the best pizza joint in town, to take back to Bea for dinner. When I ordered, and went to pay, the guy there offered me a Benny's t-shirt, saying that if I put it on and wore it that night, he'd give me my pizzas for free. I accepted the offer, though I doubt he would have got much publicity from it, me walking in the dark back to the hotel. After the pizza, we had an early night.

TUESDAY 5

I GOT UP WHILE IT was still dark and drove back down to Anglet, only to be disappointed. The line-up was a rather average-looking 3–4', with some bigger ones, but onshore as well. We were running out of time though — it was the seventh day of the waiting period and we had only completed up to the end of the second round. We were out there regardless.

I was in against American stylemaster Taylor Knox in the fifth heat of the third round. I approached the heat with caution because Taylor is a great surfer. I had a good heat, though. Taylor started with a 6.5, but then I had to wait for my wave for ages. I didn't think I was ever going to get one, but then I got a really good right and got 8.5. It really spurred me on. I heard the crew in the competitors' area clapping, and that's always a good sign. After that I only needed a few minor scores to be in touch, and I was. I had to have my wits about me though, because Taylor is so good; he can get a score from anywhere. Thankfully he didn't, often connecting with the inside only to find it bumpy and chopped up. For the first time in a few events, I'd made it past the '17th round', and I was really happy about it.

All through the day there was talk of the organisers imposing another full round on us that same day after the completion of the third round. There was a strong swell predicted for later in the week, and they obviously wanted the whole thing narrowed down to the quarter-finals so that they could feasibly move the event to Mundaka for the final day. Everyone was fairly amped on the concept, but not too many people were really too keen to surf the fourth round straight after the third. By the time we were approaching that stage, the surf had cleaned up quite a lot and was looking quite nice. However, head judge Perry Hatchett reportedly got together with Kalani Robb and C. J. Hobgood, who were drawn against each other in the first heat of round four, and they decided between them that the proposed schedule wouldn't go ahead — we'd finish the day with only round three completed.

As Damien Hobgood was going down to Shea Lopez in the last heat of round three, C. J. and Kalani had reached their decision and were kicking back at the complimentary Fosters Bar, having a few ales to wash down a hot day in the sun. Confusion followed. As word spread of the decision, some of the boys were surprised, considering the still-presentable conditions, and even more surprised to see Kalani and C. J. sucking on beers when an official call had yet to be made. The contest director blew up, and some of the Billabong people were far from impressed. A heated debate ensued before all agreed to proceed, and that the two drinking surfers' heat would be moved to the last heat of the day to give them a chance to sober up. Mind you, they were a long, long way from drunk. They'd only had one or two. In fact, both insisted that they wanted to surf their original slot as the first heat of round four. Out in the water, it seemed Kalani just couldn't take a trick, and had an absolute shocker. C. J. smashed him.

I was in heat three against Fabio Gouveia. I went for a quick free-surf down the beach before the heat, but they called me in to report before I'd done too much. The waves were bigger and cleaner than earlier in the day for round three, so I was kind of anxious about my board choice, but it felt *so* good on my first wave. I was just stoked, knowing good things were coming my way. I pretty much waxed Fabio. He got a good barrel towards the end, but he needed a 10 and didn't get it.

I was stoked that I'd made it to the quarters, and drove back to Hossegor a happy man. There was talk that the contest could be shifted to Mundaka the following day, so I was really stoked.

WEDNESDAY 6 › FRIDAY 8

MORE WAITING DAYS, *WAITING, waiting, waiting* for the promised swell. With small, rubbishy waves, these were definitely full-on 'groundhog days'. Even so, I had a few surfs. I played a little golf

too, but I mainly just hung out, relaxing and psyching for the predicted incoming swell.

One alternative activity during these three days was 'petrol-sniffing'. There was a heavy national petrol strike on, so we had to fully sniff out petrol stations that were open, had little queues, and had some diesel left, otherwise known in Europe as 'gazoil'. Diesel is really popular in Europe because petrol costs over A$2 a litre. It's heavy. Yeah, so this was a really serious petrol strike, and diesel supplies ran out first, and wouldn't you know, my Renault was a diesel. It obviously didn't help the situation that I was driving up and down the coast at this time, checking whether Anglet was breaking or not, but I had no choice. You had to be there to know what was happening.

On the Friday afternoon, word went around that the contest would resume the following day, regardless of conditions, though the promised swell was said to be on track.

SATURDAY 9

I GOT UP WAY BEFORE the dawn, and grabbed my passport in case the expected swell was really big and we had to cross the Spanish border and head to Mundaka. I got to Anglet at first light and was quite stoked to see the swell was 4–5' and clean. There was no one out there either, so I got into my wettie and paddled straight out. I got a good barrel too. They started with two girls' heats, and then it was the boys' turn.

My heat was one of the best I've ever had. My board just felt so good. I was turning it on a dime. I had Luke Hitchings, who had consistently done some nice work right through the draw. I like the way Luke surfs. He really surfs on edge and really critical. By the end of our heat though, he needed 14 points or something.

As the quarter-finals wound up, the decision was made to hold off on the semis and final and gamble on the swell rising the following day, which would enable us to go to Mundaka to finish the event. Billabong's man south of the border, Craig Sage, was reportedly betting his Mundaka home that it would be six foot down there the next morning. Like all rumours in surfing, the bet grew during the day to the point where he was betting his wife and kids as well, but I'm sure he'd never go that far. I was stoked at the potential of surfing Mundaka, but at the same time I was bummed because it meant I had to pack up all my gear and say

goodbye to Bea earlier than we'd hoped. She was heading to India early the following week. Our next stop after Mundaka would be Figueira da Foz in Portugal, and since it was a two-hour drive to Mundaka, it was logical to keep heading south after the contest in Spain had hopefully finished.

Sarge came around to get me at about 4 pm to take me down there in his car, but we didn't get too far on our first attempt. There's a one-way road next to the Mercedes, so we had to go around the block to get back to the point where we could connect with the freeway. By the time we got around the block, I realised I'd forgotten a board bag, my money and my airline tickets. I'm good at stuff like that. On the second attempt we finally got to the freeway and started heading south. After we crossed the border, heaps of the petrol stations were closed because of all the

French motorists driving down to Spain to fill up. All the way to San Sebastian we were wondering how Powelly was doing because he and Michelle had left Hossegor on an almost empty tank.

We got to Mundaka a couple of hours before dusk, found Craig Sage and booked into our little marina-side hotel. We then kicked back and had an enjoyable few beers at a little cafeteria in the park where you check the surf from. We sat there for an hour or so with Craig, Greville Mitchell, Derek O'Neill, Shane Dorian and his mum, and a few local crew that we knew who were passing by. Sunset time in Spain is like 'parade the family' time. Heaps and heaps of people come out of their houses to stroll, looking well dressed and dignified. It's good. After a few beers, Sarge and I had dinner with Greville and Lisa, which was great, and then we had an early night.

SUNDAY 10

LAST DAY OF THIS BOOK! I woke up super-early, way before first light, and could hear the surf rumbling, but I was really anxious about whether it really had risen and was good, or whether we had to drive all the way back to Anglet to finish the job. It finally cracked first light, and I was stoked. It was a solid five foot, and it looked perfect. I was jumping around. I ran down to get out there, but then I decided against an early surf because I was in the first heat, the first semi-final. By that stage it was about 8 am.

I paddled out knowing that C. J. Hobgood was going to be the toughest heat. We both got nines for kind of smaller but really good barrels. I was in the lead but then he came up with a 9.5 right at the end, and pegged me. I was stressing, thinking, 'Oh no!' I thought it was over. Right at the end I heard Shane Dorian screaming as he was paddling out for his semi-final. I was wondering what he was on about, but then I paddled over a wave and there was this bigger wave there. 'No way!' I thought. I was stoked. C. J. was frothing but I just turned around and didn't even really paddle, just slipped right into it, straight into the barrel.

I got really deep, and I was in the barrel thinking, 'I only need a 7.25, but this is such a 10!' Everything kind of slowed down and I was talking to myself, going, 'Oh my God, this barrel is just so beautiful' I'll always remember it. I gave it a couple of pumps and just came flying out of it. It was one of the highlights of my career, just being way back in that barrel, so long, so deep. It was like winning the jackpot. My caddy Craig paddled straight up to me and said, 'That was unbelievable.'

'Yeah, that was a 10, hey?' was all I could say.

Sure enough, the announcer called out '10!' and everyone was just hooting and screaming. It was such a good feeling.

Maybe I got too excited. Maybe I should have just tried to contain myself and win the final, but I went straight back out for the final after Shane had beaten Willsy in the second semi. I actually thought there was an expression session between the semis and the final, and I was scoffing a few croissants when Sunny Garcia said to me, 'Don't eat too much, you've got to go straight back out.' I gave Sunny one of the croissants, and he loved it. They put honey on them down there in the Basque country. They're beautiful. I ran off to get my board.

I felt really confident that I'd win, but the very first set Shane suckered me into a medium-sized one. He said, 'Are you going Occ?' I looked at it, and I wasn't going to, but I thought 'Yeah' and I went, because I was on the inside. I fell off in the barrel and that was just not good. Shane then got a good wave, and after that I just couldn't seem to do anything right. I fell off something like seven times a row in the barrel. But anyway, I was stoked to be in the final, and stoked to have got through the heat with C. J. and get that 10, so it was good.

We had a fantastic traditional Basque presentation ceremony—they threw Shane in the harbour, as they did to me last year after I'd won. Then Willsy, Beau, Jake Pato, Hitcho, Sarge, our Brazilian mate Fernando, Navrin Fox and his girl, and I just sat around outside our hotel, chinwagging and drinking beers. It was a big day. That was about it. We got up the following morning and convoyed to Figueira Da Foz, a two-hour drive north of Lisbon in Portugal for the next event. Onward we roll!

THE REMAINDER OF 2000 ...

BETWEEN FINISHING THE RECORDINGS for this book, we had surfed the Figueira Pro WCT in Portugal, and I lost early. I thought the water would be colder than it turned out to be and wore too thick a wetsuit, which restricted me a bit. I had too many falls. I wanted to back up and do well, but it just didn't happen. I've had such an inconsistent season, going up and down like a yo-yo in just about everything. It's been a good year, though. It's certainly been interesting.

The next event is the Billabong Pro at Trestles and I'm really looking forward to it. It's a really high-performance wave. After that we go back to Brazil where I won the world title last year, so that will have special significance. From there we actually get a few weeks back at home before heading over to Hawaii in early November for the Triple Crown, which includes the last WCT of the season, the Pipeline Masters. I can't wait!

Other great surfing titles from Harper*Sports*

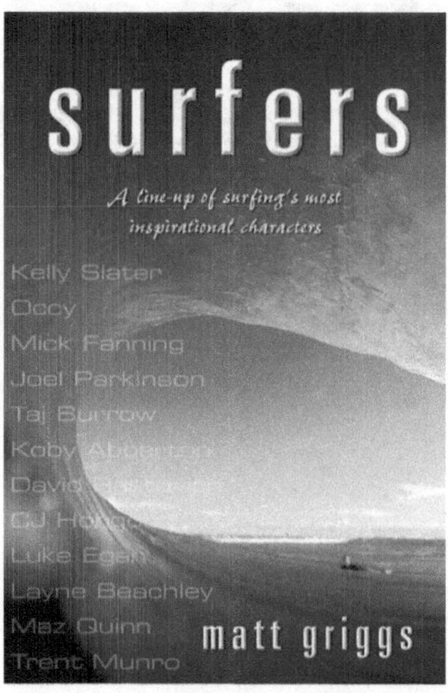
surfers
A line-up of surfing's most inspirational characters
Kelly Slater
Occy
Mick Fanning
Joel Parkinson
Taj Burrow
Koby
David
CJ
Luke
Layne Beachley
Maz Quinn
Trent Munro
matt griggs

SURFERS

Matt Griggs

Jump in the V8s of Mick Fanning, Joel Parkinson and Dean Morrison in Coolangatta. Stroke into a set at Waimea Bay with Kieren Perrow. Have breakfast with current world champion CJ Hobgood and seven other former world champions in Newcastle. Go on a spiritual adventure with David Rastovich in Peru. Enjoy a country beer with Trent Munro at Scotts Head. Learn of Koby Abberton's hard – and softer – side at Maroubra. Encounter the surfing culture of Brazil and New Zealand with Neco Padaratz and Maz Quinn. Spend a weekend with Mark Occhilupo in his old stomping ground of Cronulla. Survive a near-death experience at G-Land with Luke Egan. Get inside the creative minds of Oscar Wright and photographer Jon Frank. Relive the ten-year surfing odyssey of Peter Troy and tag along in the youthful exploits of Luke Munro. Cheer one of the world's least accomplished professional surfers, Wade Glasscock, and admire the world's best, Kelly Slater. And wonder at Taj Burrow's legendary prowess with the ladies . . .

In *Surfers*, former professional surfer and *Tracks* writer Matt Griggs gives an insider's view of a line-up of surfing's most interesting and unique characters. At turns funny and sad but always inspiring, it lifts the lid on one of the world's most dynamic, enigmatic and mysterious sports.

ISBN 0 7322 7485 0

mark warren's
Atlas
of Australian
SURFING
the original surf guide
traveller's edition

ATLAS OF AUSTRALIAN SURFING: TRAVELLER'S EDITION

Mark Warren

From the warm, clear water and unforgettable waves of far north Queensland to the cold and unforgiving swells of eastern Tasmania, *Atlas of Australian Surfing: Traveller's Edition* provides the most complete state-by-state guide to all the great surf breaks around Australia's coastline.

A former world and Australian champion, Mark Warren has been surfing the great Australian breaks since he was a grommet growing up in Sydney. Now his 30 years of experience and knowledge have been distilled into the new traveller's edition of his bestselling guide to the Australian surfing scene.

Atlas of Australian Surfing: Traveller's Edition offers a whole new range of surfing possibilities for those prepared to travel a little further than their local break.

It's much more than an adventure. It's an odyssey.

ISBN 0 7322 6731 5

new edition of the cult classic
'articulate, personable
calculating & stylish,
Rabbit defines an era of
innovation and individuality.'
— Kelly Slater
wayne Rabbit bartholomew
bustin'
down the
door
with
tim baker

BUSTIN' DOWN THE DOOR

Wayne 'Rabbit' Bartholomew with Tim Baker

From street urchin to world surfing champion to boardroom heavyweight, this new and revised edition of the bestselling cult classic captures all the intrigue and adventure of Wayne 'Rabbit' Bartholomew's remarkable personal journey.

World Champion in 1978, World Masters Champion in 1999, and currently CEO/President of the ASP, Rabbit's charisma, flamboyance and warrior spirit have helped define surfing over three decades.

ISBN 0 7322 7479 6

www.ingramcontent.com/pod-product-compliance
Lightning Source LLC
Chambersburg PA
CBHW061555100726
47898CB00002B/386

* 9 7 8 0 7 3 2 2 6 8 5 5 8 *